DEDICATION

The making of a book is rarely the work of one individual.

More importantly is the making of the life of the author, which is formed by the many people who impacted, influenced, and helped to mold the vessel into what it should be.

It is then the author, out of that life experience, who has the responsibility and privilege to convey a meaningful message to the people.

God has used wonderful people in my life to bring me personally into a new dimension of emotional health and wholeness. It is to them and all the servants in "Helping Professions" that this book is dedicated. May you be strengthened and go forward boldly in your work.

God loves every person who is experiencing any type of emotional pain or distress. It is to those in the process of healing and recovery that I dedicate this book. **God is with you more than you know.**

CONTENTS

ACKNOWLEDGMENTS

Thanks to Sara Jirik, the first person whose testimony of wholeness and personal change made me hungry and open to do my own emotional work.

• • •

Blessings to the person whose closeness and unique gift richly enhanced my life. Sometimes unknown to you, your presence forced me to face myself and my issues. You taught me how to relax, how to enjoy nurturing and have fun, and you created a safe place for me to rest and heal. God used you and I will always be thankful.

• • •

Thanks to Dr. David Eide and Dr. Mike McGowan for pointing me in the right direction and getting me started.

• • •

I express my heartfelt gratitude to Ariel White-Kovach and Karen Finck – "healers" in the true sense of the word. Thank you for your patience, honesty, love, and understanding that has touched my life in a deep and special way. I consider you among my mentors. Your work has changed my life and I pray that through me, will now touch many others.

• • •

My thanks to the unique people of Twin Cities Harvest Church for giving me the privilege to pastor you. Our experiences together have created a chapter in my life that will always be beautiful and precious. For that, you have a special place in my heart. All the best!

• • •

Denyse Cummings, it's great that you heard God, responded so quickly, and have topped the challenge of the message. You do great work and I appreciate you. Thanks!

INTRODUCTION

This is a book about discovery and healing. It's about allowing God to meet you in a profound, personal way. In these pages I want to take you with me into a very serious spiritual search. We will go into the private, inner areas of the heart of man, where things are going on that we don't always want to talk about.

This book is not intended to be a definitive work on emotions. It is not intended for just one gender. Nor is it intended to present a psychological personality theory. What you find here has helped me embrace truth during a transitional season in my own life. Furthermore, I know God has spoken to me of the necessity of this message as part of the preparation and maturing of His end-time church. I don't believe that healing toxic emotions is for everyone; and it is not a requirement for being spiritual or walking closely with God.

My goal in writing is to present a **simplified** and **basic** understanding about the place of emotional wholeness in the life of a believer. It is to present ideas that may open a door to some new thoughts for you that could propel you forward into new dimensions of Christian growth and start you in the healing process. I also want to assist you in finding quality of life as a person. I offer no superquick fixes, no surefire guarantees, and no airtight solutions.

At times I have thought my presentation was too simple; but the Lord continually took me back to my uncomplicated goal. I must proclaim continued healing, deliverance, holiness, maturity, and soundness for the body of Christ. My desire for this book is to be a VOICE.

I can relate to a statement made by Keith Miller in his book, The Secret Life of the Soul. He said, "*A number of people have told me recently that somehow the spiritual adventure, and life in general, have gone dead for them, that their faith has not been able to solve their inner difficulties. They turn their problems over to God, but God seems to leave them untouched. They don't know whether this is due to the inadequacy of their faith or to their own inability to deal with their lives and relationships. Many people, through spiritual groups in church, through the twelve-step programs, and in counselling sessions, have realized there's a previously undiscovered level of life going on inside themselves.*"[1]

I absolutely support the idea that God is using new avenues like support groups in the church, et cetera; not to necessarily replace old methods but to add to what we already have and to bring us into a rich dimension of wholeness. For me, experiencing a new level of emotional wholeness has been challenging, yet sensational!

My hope is that you will somehow see yourself in my story, which may seem very trite, or in some parts, very extreme; but points to the drama of the warfare that can go on inside a deep spiritual mind and heart. I have mined my own experiences from a life dedicated to seeking God, and have found some very powerful answers.

Your story may be much more tragic, laced with abuse and horrific heartache. Maybe you are well-adjusted and have been relatively happy all through life. All of our stories are unique, and all of us have met God in special ways. For many, <u>Healing Toxic Emotions</u> will open the door to a special experience with a loving and powerful God. I have tried to paint a very simple picture for you of how you can easily find God in allowing Him to heal your emotions. I hope you can relate somewhere, and suspend your skepticism to be open to a new way of thinking and a new experience of faith and hope. I urge you to take this book at your own pace and on your own terms. I want you to know God is with you as you read. You may not find everything agreeable or applicable, but something here is bound to grace your life.

The soul realm, the emotions, will always be a bit mysterious; but as each of us encounter God in our unique spiritual journeys, He always seems to make personal and individual sense of the things that aren't always humanly easy to understand. He is so good!

May God bless you and change your life as you read <u>Healing Toxic Emotions: *The Battle For Your True Identity*</u>.

Mary Alice Isleib
Eden Prairie, Minnesota

Chapter I

IN THE BEGINNING...SHAME

The Bible doesn't talk about shame, an emotion, very often. But when the word *is* mentioned, it's very powerful. Let's read in the book of the Bible that is called, "The Book of Beginnings" – the book of Genesis – and study how shame was first introduced into the earth.

In Genesis 1:26, we can read where God said,

"Let us make man in our image, after our likeness. ..."

The verse goes on to describe some of the godlike attributes that would be given to mankind: dominion, fruitfulness, a blessed life. As believers, most of us are very familiar with that portion of our spiritual, emotional, and physical heritage from God.

Now I want you to notice another portion of our godly inheritance that some of us have missed. In chapter two, man was created and God called him Adam; then He made woman. I want you to particularly notice what God says about them in Genesis 2:25.

"And they were both naked, the man and his wife, and were not ashamed."

Believers like to emphasize that through the Lord, we were given dominion and that we're blessed. We exercise spiritual dominion through our prayer life, our Christian lifestyles, and our God-inspired words that when spoken by the unction of God, will change situations to bring Him glory.

But we have failed to recognize that another attribute of His blessing upon mankind was that we were to feel *no shame*.

The scripture says that Adam and Eve were not ashamed. The emotion of shame was in its right perspective and in its proper order in their lives. I believe they felt healthy shame, but they did not bear any poisonous or toxic shame, or any other toxic emotions either.

When the scripture says they were naked, it speaks of a transparency. God intended for us to have a sense of security and originality, without walls or defenses. He created us to live vulnerable, sound, and pure in a Biblical way, with nothing to hide. He wants us to be so comfortable with ourselves that we are not afraid to be easily seen, clear, and obvious concerning who we are. God didn't intend for us just to live that way physically – but emotionally and mentally as well.

Adam and Eve lived in the midst of the garden, *without shame*, clothed with *dominion, fruitfulness*, and *blessings*. In this level of environment, Adam and Eve created a nurturing, loving, and healthy emotional life, creating a flourishing, sound relationship.

OUR IDENTITY WAS ESTABLISHED

The emotion of shame that is mentioned here in the book of Beginnings – the book of Genesis – is an "**identity**" **emotion**. As Christian identities were established by God in this book, we must understand that a life free from shame is a part of our identity and spiritual heritage. Just as we understand our identity through Jesus Christ as we exercise *spiritual dominion* and live in the fruitfulness of it, we are also designed to have an emotional life free from the plaguing feelings of excess, toxic shame.

Because shame is an emotion that causes you to feel something about yourself – who you are and what you are as a person – it is closely tied to your identity. Many times we accept what shame tells us about ourselves or a part of our lives, that isn't based on truth, but on a feeling that can be so strong, yet so silent, you aren't even aware that it's speaking to you. When you are living free from toxic shame, you are transparent, vulnerable, and open with others. Your freedom allows you to show the true identity of who you are, what you believe, what your feelings are, what your needs are, and where your trust is. You are totally free to be yourself. If you are living with toxic shame, you can subtly feel that something is morally and almost lethally wrong with you, that you will always be a failure as a person, or in a specific area of your life. You want to hide yourself so others won't see the real you or your shame. There is an unconscious dynamic where shame speaks to you as a feeling; a bad, dark, empty feeling; a "void" inside. It convinces you that if people saw you *as you felt*, it would be unbearable. It makes you feel seen in an exposed way. Toxic shame degrades who you are as a person – your identity. So do toxic emotions.

As we continue in our study, remember that shame is an emotion that is closely tied to your true personhood – your core identity. Most of the other emotions tell you how you are to react or relate to circumstances or to others. But shame tells you something about *yourself.*

SIN ESTABLISHED A FALSE IDENTITY

We all know how the story of Adam and Eve, through a process of events, came to a very sad conclusion; but I want to point out a few things about them. Before sin came in, they were absolutely and totally shame-free, weren't they? There was no need for masks. They weren't in pain emotionally, spiritually or physically, because they were free before each other and one with God. They enjoyed their good emotions, managed the bad emotions, and for a time, avoided the sinful ones. They had true, transparent intimacy with each other and the same intimacy with God.

Adam and Eve's emotions were given to them by God. At first, they knew what emotions were for and they understood how to manage them. Their emotions weren't tarnished by sin.

Well, you know the story. The serpent came in and the couple fell from their place with God.

I want you to read the following verse very slowly. It tells of a significant thing that happened once they fell.

"And the eyes of them both were opened, and they knew that they were naked..."

Genesis 3:7

What God wants us to see, is that the results of sin made them aware that they were emotionally vulnerable. Their identities were marred by the bad feelings they had about themselves, and then they groped for cover-ups to medicate that feeling. The covers immediately became a part of their personality – their identity – all to get away from the influence of excess shame.

How do you feel when you're shamed? You can feel like, "Ooh, ah; everyone sees me." Everyone does not see you, but the feeling of shame is a feeling of extreme vulnerability, isn't it?

God has given shame as an emotion that moves us to things like repentance and modesty. But when sin came in, that shame became perverted to a toxic shame. It became an

4

unhealthy emotion that was a part of the curse.

Suddenly, Adam and Eve both realized they were naked and what happened? They became ashamed. The Taylor translation says they were embarrassed.

A "COVER" INVENTED BY SIN

The Bible speaks very clearly about how they *felt*. It doesn't speak of a spiritual concept. And, it doesn't speak of other emotions like sadness or depression; it clearly speaks of the experience of shame. The Scriptures say they were very aware and ashamed. Look what happened next.

"...and they sewed fig leaves together, and made themselves aprons."

What did they do? They sewed fig leaves together to do what? **Cover themselves.** What does shame want you to do? **Hide. Run. Get out of sight.**

We've just read that it's a scriptural concept for shame to want to hide.

Sometimes shame wants to stay hidden from your eyes so that you don't see, even in your own private motivations and behaviors that can be shaming or shamed-based. We've shut-out some areas of our lives for so long, that we're not even aware that God is wanting to come in those places and set us free; not just from the spiritual roots of our own issues, but from the negative, empty *feelings* created by toxic shame. **The only way that shame is healed is if it's brought into the light.** Shame must be named. The devil will try to keep shame hidden; but God wants to bring it to light so that it can be healed. When it is hidden, it can't be worked out.

Hiding was not the end of the story for Adam and Eve. It got worse; their shame became toxic.

THE SOURCE OF BROKEN RELATIONSHIPS

"And they heard the voice of the Lord God walking in the garden in the cool of the day: and Adam and his wife hid themselves from the presence of the Lord God amongst the trees of the garden."

Verse 8

Follow this pattern with me. Sin brought shame. The shame became unhealthy and the couple tried to hide themselves. Now the shame became chronic or toxic, because it has broken their relationship with God. Adam and Eve felt such an intense, internal shame that it separated them from God.

On the subject of relationships, some specialists believe that the reason many friendships and marriages don't make it may be because of an unhealthy shame embedded in one of the partners.

Adam and Eve now had a broken relationship with God. I wonder if their relationship with each other was broken. I believe that it was because as we'll read later, Adam began to blame Eve for the trouble. I also believe that Adam and Even started fighting. Can you imagine it — fighting in the midst of the beautiful utopia? Now you can begin to see just how very ugly shame truly is.

"And the Lord called unto Adam, and said unto him, Where art thou?"

Verse 9

Just as shame broke their connection with God, shame will not allow you to connect with people. It won't allow you to be vulnerable to show your true self and to have a deep, trusting relationship. Excess shame can become so strong that to some it means that whenever there is a feeling of any type, any need, any drive, they imme-

6

diately feel ashamed. That's why it is so important to heal it, so the other emotions can follow.

Shame won't allow you to fully connect and become intimate with God either. God loves you and wants to be with you. But when we are filled with chronic shame, the devil whispers to us that God doesn't even want us – and we believe it! Or, we hear that God loves us, but we still have to *feel* bad about something. So we carry around this prevailing feeling of sorrow inside, even when we go to God and experience His fullness. It's called shame.

I think the preceding verses are very sad, and illustrate just some of the ways shame can become toxic to your life. Did you read where God called out for Adam? Yet, shame made Adam and Eve hide themselves from the One who loved them most, thinking they weren't wanted by Him or that they couldn't relate to Him. Now we have not just a spiritual crisis, but an emotional one as well because of shame. How very, very sad.

FEAR, MASKS, AND BLAME

"And he said, I heard thy voice in the garden, and I was afraid, because I was naked; and I hid myself."

Verse 10

Do you see what came in next because of excess shame? Fear. Adam is hiding, and now he is afraid. He is harboring deep-seeded fears, and is somehow becoming more and more spiritually and emotionally paralyzed.

"And he said, Who told thee that thou wast naked?"

Verse 11

In other words, God bluntly asked, "Adam, who told you that you were ashamed?" Remember friends, the heart of God doesn't want us to participate with unhealthy shame.

God's heart is that we not be bound by toxic shame. He was saying, "You're supposed to be vulnerable and free! Who told you that you were naked?"

When God asked them such a heartfelt question, instead of answering honestly, Adam and Eve put on a mask. They turned into people they weren't supposed to be. Suddenly pride and arrogance entered their world. They became the center of attention in their own world, selfish, lonely, and power-hungry.

Let's keep reading in verse ten.

"Hast thou eaten of the tree, whereof I commanded thee that thou shouldest not eat?"

Here comes Adam's response behind his new found mask.

"And the man said, The woman whom thou gavest to be with me, she gave me of the tree, and I did eat."

Verse 11

There's another attribute of shame – the cover-up called blame. We're going to discuss this later in the book, but you're going to see that **blame is one of the most powerful covers for hiding and trying to medicate the feelings shame produces.** Shame is in the art of blame.

A shamed person refuses to take responsibility because the shame makes them feel desperately bad and anxious about who they are. Instead, shame projects the fault upon someone else to protect itself from the uncomfortable feeling. The best thing that Adam could have done was to have admitted the truth. But he didn't; and we have a cycle of toxic shame and its fruit that began way back in the garden.

Chapter 2

THE LITTLE GRAY CLOUD
My Personal Testimony

I couldn't stand it any longer. I had to ask. "Have you noticed that lately I've been depressed?"

My secretary was surprised and a little taken back to hear me ask such a vulnerable question. I think she was a little concerned that her job might be on the line if she crossed my private boundaries and answered truthfully. But thank God, she went past any feelings of fear that she might have had.

Pausing before an answer, she replied, "Ah, well, you know Mary Alice, I have been praying for you. I've noticed that there *is* a gray cloud that comes to the office with you sometimes. I'm used to seeing you bold in your ministry; but when that lifts, you've got some depression and sadness that hangs around in your everyday life."

Ah, there it was – the confirmation from another person of what I already knew to be true.

I HAD SEEN IT ALL

I had always thought that I had it together. God wasn't the problem. He had always been there. The anointing was strong in my ministry, sometimes stronger than I could handle. I was used to speaking and lecturing to crowds, large and small, sometimes for hours on end. I was accustomed to standing before nations and addressing evil principalities; I had seen thousands come to the Lord. I had helped start churches in the tougher portions of the European Eastern Bloc and in Russia. I had been privileged to be a missionary in Sweden, taking an active role in a great church there, teaching in its Bible Center and directing its prayer school. It was nothing for the rebels of that nation to plant bombs outside the church doors, or for us to receive death threats if we continued to evangelize and propagate the gospel throughout Scandinavia, Russia, and the Eastern Bloc.

As a single woman, I had traveled extensively throughout North America, Europe, Asia, and the South Pacific, as an international speaker on effective fervent prayer. I love prayer. I knew how to pray. I was accustomed to strength, both physically and spiritually. Now I had returned stateside to begin a church in Minneapolis. I had surmounted all the usual persecution that comes with starting anything new. I gathered the sheep, won the lost, established the administration for the church, set the leadership, and preached every week while maintaining a strong itinerant ministry schedule. I had learned to adapt myself to hard or difficult situations. The gifts God had given me were working well.

So what was this nagging "gray cloud" that suddenly kept hanging around me when I was alone?

MORE PROBLEMS

You must know that before I dared to ask my secretary if she thought I might be depressed, I had done everything I knew to do. I mean, I was "the prayer lady," the woman of great strength and power! The prayer lady couldn't struggle with persistent, unpleasant, and sometimes dark, empty feelings inside. Surely I knew how to handle it.

I had prayed until I was weak and there was nothing

left in me to pray. I had cast if off me and cast it out of me until there was nothing left that I knew to cast. I praised God with dancing and shouting until I was so exhausted I couldn't dance anymore.

But the little gray cloud remained.

On Sunday mornings, I always felt great. I was focused in my message, and strong in the power of the Lord. My itinerant schedule kept me hopping airplanes, meeting lots of people, and preaching in the nations. It was wonderful when I was engulfed in a project or on the go. In fact, I'd really enjoy the pulpit because I felt great when I was operating in my gift! But as soon as I left the place where I was gifted and comfortable, as soon as I found myself alone without a flight to catch or a project to work on, the gray cloud came back.

As if the plaguing gray cloud wasn't enough, I also began to have stomach problems. I went to a medical physician and a nutritionist, kept regular appointments, took medicine, and purchased every kind of herbal treatment imaginable. I took every kind of test that I could go through, and each test returned normal. I knew some of it was a spiritual attack, but I realized something else had to be wrong. At times, the stomach problems seemed to get better; but nonetheless persisted. No matter what sort of treatment I sought, it seemed nothing totally helped me.

During this period of time, I was also in a serious relationship that was leading to marriage. I dearly loved this man for many reasons; but during the pre-marital counseling, we broke off the engagement. Aside from my physical problems, I was in tremendous emotional pain and turmoil over losing another relationship. I was sad, confused, and hurting. I had had enough.

I REBUKE YOU, SATAN!

Regardless, I kept doing what I knew to do. After one of the visits to the nutritionist, he finally said to me, "Mary Alice, I've given you many kinds of treatment. You've made some improvement, but the problems still persist. I think you're dealing with some emotional issues here. There are many ways to healing, and you should explore other avenues. Have you ever considered seeing a counselor? You need someone to ask you the right questions that will help to locate what is going on in your heart. I think you will find some answers there about what your stomach is so bothered about."

I thought, "I rebuke you, Satan! I'm not talking to anyone! I don't need help. That is for the weak, or the really desperate people. I mean, I'm a leader in the body of Christ – how dare you give me that nice advice!"

Six months later, the problems still persisted. Finding only periodic relief, I began to mull over the suggestion that my nutritionist had given me. Maybe he had some thoughts that I should prayerfully consider. I wasn't in a clinical depression; I wasn't suicidal or anything like that. I didn't need medication. I just wanted the nagging gray cloud and the physical discomforts to be gone from my life. I needed answers, so I began to pray differently.

"God," I earnestly pleaded, "what *is* this? What's wrong with me? Why can't I get healed? Why do I feel separated from the hearts of the members of my church? Why can't I have fulfilling relationships with some of my colleagues? Why can't I connect with the people closest to me? Why do I still struggle with some bad habits and unhealthy behaviors? There are some things I'm feeling about myself that I don't like. God, I need help."

From that serious time of prayer, God began to lead me down a surprising path – a path of **learning to identify and manage my emotions,** a path of self-discovery. A path of understanding what healthy relationships are. A path of healing areas of toxic shame in my soul. A path of emotional and mental wholeness.

I looked for in-depth reading material on this subject written by Christians, but could find very little, especially from charismatic circles. I read many good secular books on the subject. With those books, I learned what applied to me and agreed with my value system, and disregarded the rest. To my surprise, I started to learn truths that I didn't know, or had never dared to pursue or tried to understand. I began to seek God in a new way, and also to seek the help of others. God led me to the right people and the right place at just the right time, who ministered to me and taught me a completely new dimension of wholeness and deliverance.

TIME TO GET REAL

Healing toxic emotions was a totally different experience from anything I've been used to. I was used to applying Bible verses and was well-versed at the "spiritual" side of coping with life's problems. I was relatively open to talking with qualified and knowledgeable people, including God - or so I thought. But I had to take a new step of faith and open up the emotional part of my life to different people - safe and supportive individuals with whom I talked with face-to-face, for several hours at a time, describing what was really going on in the depths of my heart – both the good and the bad, the past and the present. It was a time of self-disclosure. I openly discussed feelings and experiences you sometimes don't even get the chance to explore yourself, much less within the tender conversations in the most intimate relationships of your life. I had to ruthlessly and honestly examine my fears, problems, reactions, family background, and relationships, as well as my successes. I had to dare speak of my worst fears, to be rigorously honest and vulnerable; which isn't easy in our society, including the church world. I explored my deepest emotions. I wasn't used to going there, even though I thought I was. It can be scary and uncomfortable because of its unknown elements; but it's very important to allow God to help you open up that place of self-awareness in your life. God is there! And so is your true identity.

One of the things I found is that the spirit, soul, and body are very closely tied together. For example, your mind won't stay clear if your emotions aren't healed or your body is constantly tired. It's hard to stay spiritually strong if you are alone and don't know how to relate or bond with people. It's hard to stay mentally and emotionally well without taking the time to develop and keep a strong spiritual life. You can be really healthy in your body, and then have a distressing emotional or relational experience take your health away. Experts in all fields are proving daily that physical health and emotional health are very closely tied together. You can't ignore one at the expense of the other. When one area isn't functioning in a wholesome manner, the other areas suffer.

I discovered that I had unknowingly ignored some realms of emotion in my life. Let's face it, we haven't been taught much and many times, not taught well about the emotional arena. As you will learn, we must gain knowledge in order to function properly here. I discovered that with a willingness to be honest with ourselves, and a little under-standing of what emotions are and how they operate, that wholeness can come and begin its work.

On the surface, I was a happy Christian, a good friend, daughter, and sister, operating in my gifts and calling, serving the church. But in my private life, in some areas of my emotional life, I was bound. That's why I was experiencing the symptoms in my physical body. I prayed like David prayed in Psalm 139, "Lord, let me know truth in my inward parts; search me and know me. Try me and see if there be any anxieties in my life." That heartfelt honesty led me on a very powerful life-changing journey.

On this journey, God did a very deep work in me, and continues to do so. He took me inside of my heart, the inside of my being, and spoke with me concerning the healing of toxic emotions.

I realized that over the many years of successful public ministry, and through many battles, most of which were won victoriously by God's grace, there were things going on inside of me that I had never gotten in touch with. I wasn't rebellious or unwilling to look at them. But sometimes the battle was so great and there were so many people to deal with and schedules to keep, that I just didn't take the time to always completely process what was going on in my soul when the attacks and common affairs of life met me. I knew I was strong in the Lord. I knew I was bold and that the anointing would take care of me. I knew I was delivered; but I was ignorant concerning the healthy habits of a prosperous and sound emotional life. Now there were issues that needed to be uncovered, understood, and faced. There were areas of healing and understanding that God wanted to give me in a new and fresh way.

NO "DRIVE-THROUGH" HEALINGS

The journey was very difficult. In fact, throughout all the exciting and difficult exploits of my life, gaining emotional wholeness was one of the most challenging exercises and lessons I have ever been through. It was scary for me at first, because in the body of Christ we're not used to – sometimes not supposed to – even discuss emotional wholeness, nor do we have to connect with ourselves or others in order to heal. For some reason, we'd rather believe for the instantaneous miracles or ignore our situation, hoping it will go away. We want someone to lay hands on us, pray for us, and everything be rosy for the rest of our lives. We don't want to work toward wholeness. It's hard work, and besides, most of us don't think we need it. At first, I didn't think I needed it either! But, God had me obey and trust Him. In so doing, He gently and lovingly proved me wrong.

I'm not going to lead you to believe that some anointed person came and whacked me on top of the head and all my problems were zapped. I love the joy of the Lord, but I didn't laugh my way to freedom in the aisles of a church. No one prayed for me over the telephone, then expected me to come and give a testimony of instantaneous deliverance.

No, my healing was a process. Working with my humility, He would shine His light upon me, even in the times when the road seemed very dark and hopeless. God was always there and He will be for you too. Unresolved disappointments surfaced that I had suppressed for years upon end. I realized that I was carrying a lot of emotions that were stuck; they weren't operating the right way, or weren't even processed at all. It wasn't because I didn't want to process them. It was because the intensity of the battle was at times so severe and lengthy, and the affairs of life so busy and challenging, that I didn't know *how* to process them and survive.

So unintentionally, I buried my true feelings and didn't connect with God or myself at the time. Therefore, I accumulated some emotional baggage. It seemed a bit strange to me, because I had a relatively normal Christian upbringing, and a fairly healthy life. In fact, I'm sure that you have probably been through many more difficult and tough things than I have; but whatever the case, we all need to get well. I obviously did not properly understand the course of emotions in life's circumstances, and the ignorance of it created pain and lack within me. My spiritual enemies were taking advantage of those things and warring against me. After awhile, those repeated, unresolved issues began to show up in my physical body. Now was my time to deal with them.

Sometimes when Christians or people in general have unresolved, internal issues – such as emotional pain, embarrassment, disappointments, failure, pride, and selfishness – they point fingers to blame or they backslide. I didn't feel like doing that. Instead, I internalized a lot of thoughts and feelings that I later understood in my time of self-examination.

For instance, I had lost some precious and valuable relationships at different times in my life. Years later, I understood that I was continuing to grieve those losses. My mind wasn't consciously aware of the grief and my spirit was clear of all unforgiveness in it, but the grief kept passing through my soul. Suddenly, I realized that I didn't know the first thing of how to grieve properly. Instead, I had pushed those sorrows and feelings somewhere into the depths of my being and just went on "serving the Lord." After all, I was in an "army," bent to serve, paying no attention to how I felt.

Some of the places I found in my heart were a surprise to me. I had experienced healing and deliverance in the past, but I didn't know the root of some of the more recent problems I was experiencing. I had only tasted some of the bitter fruit, and I was tired of it. There were places that were tender, bruised, and sensitive. There were portions of my heart that were filled with toxic shame. I also discovered that with this shame that was alive within me, I was concerned, afraid, or nervous about what other people were going to think if the shame was uncovered.

That's what God wanted; a discovery, a cleansing, and healing. There were hardened areas that were crusty with pride, defensiveness, denial, stubbornness, and rebellion. God wanted to reveal that part of my ego to me, and clean it up as well.

I found myself wanting to hide and protect these secret places. Hiding was against my character because I'm an honest and good lady, I love people, and I love to be used by Lord. But God was ready again to allow me to know His love and grace as I have known it so powerfully before. God wanted me to stop hiding from *Him*.

ARE YOU THRIVING IN ALL THINGS?

Like countless others, I had always heard it taught in Bible class that we shouldn't be led by our feelings. **That statement is only a half-truth.** Like countless others, I also went to the extreme thinking somehow that if I couldn't be led by emotions, then emotions must be bad. Or just as worse, that emotions must be ignored or suppressed (especially the negative ones), or that we should just "get out of our feelings and go on."

I understand that line of thinking, as most people are dominated by their emotions (whether they show it or not), and they need to grow up, make the right decisions, and move on. All these lines of thinking are good and necessary when applied in the proper cases. But for many people, the true healing comes when they are allowed to do just the contrary - feel the feelings.

Third John 2 amply states a significant key to thriving in all areas of our lives. The writer says,

"Beloved, I wish above all things that thou mayest prosper (thrive in all things) *and be in health, even as thy SOUL prospereth* (thrives)."

I have learned that healed emotions are vital and very important to being sound; so much so, that they cannot be suppressed or ignored. We are not to be led by them, become trapped in them, or make decisions based on them. But our feelings must be recognized, acknowledged, explored, and understood before we can thrive in life. This art is so accurately called "Emotional Intelligence" and I was lacking in it.

That little gray cloud had ground to stay around me, because I had ignored the health of my soul. I wasn't intentionally trying to hide anything. Some of my emotions were hidden from *me* because I had buried them so deeply. Some of my emotions were impaired by my not knowing what I was really experiencing, how it works, or what it was even for. Other emotions were numbed or present in excess due to something called toxic shame, which I will concentrate on later.

One by one, God began to shine His light on each area. He touched them, healed them, and set me free from wounds, bondage, shame, hardness, and insecurities. He showed me my negative traits and how to manage them effectively. Praise God! It's been one of the greatest deliverances I have ever experienced. My life and ministry has been revolutionized.

Chapter 3

DISPELLING THE MYTHS
OF THE MESSAGE

I've found a new peace with myself and God. I'm able to be more intimate with God and with others. I am able to be more transparent and more real before the congregations that I minister to. I'm learning that I no longer have to protect or defend my insecurities, or myself. I don't have to try to prove myself to anyone anymore, including God Himself. I can be genuine, open, and generous because I have become more of who I am. I've discovered that I don't have to allow shame, insecurity, or any kind of inner pain to separate me from the people of God, or from anyone for that matter. I've learned to handle it properly when people around me are being goofy, dysfunctional, or power-hungry, so that it doesn't affect me. I am learning what healthy relationships are and how to establish good boundaries. I'm learning how to live sound, secure, and emotionally healthy. Praise God!

As emotional intelligence became clear to me, the Lord said, **"You've got to teach My people how to stay well emotionally, because the experiences of life in the 21st Century will bring a need for revelation, restoration, and healing in this area."**

Among other things, I began to realize that if we, as ministers and believers, push down, ignore, refuse to manage unhealthy emotions, or lack the knowledge to let them take their proper course, then we will become ineffective in some way or another – abusive, power-hungry, depressed, or sick, just to name a few. Unless we as believers understand how to work with our souls, we can never completely fulfill the plan of God for our lives. Besides being unfulfilled, or constantly physically ill, we will also leave a trail of broken, shattered lives strewn along the wayside that we have hurt because of our own selfish, soulish dysfunction. God dearly loves His people; and He won't take it lightly when His people are mistreated or abused by others, no matter what the excuse.

EXCUSES AREN'T POPULAR WITH GOD

Emotions aren't easy to talk about. First of all, we just plain "don't want to get too emotional." Another problem with being vulnerable, transparent, and open about your emotions is that there's always the danger that in your exposed state, someone will use you, alienate you, or talk about you. In some cases that has happened because we, as believers, haven't learned how to be "safe" people and create a supportive, non-judgmental environment where others can genuinely open up, talk about, and deal with their issues, then heal.

Many times it's easier to ignore the soulish realm, because it "just gets too messy," or could get out of control. After all, we don't want to become a "hospital" or a "baby-sitting service." It's much easier to say, "People should just grow up and get over it."

We have developed such anxiety over wanting to look good before others, wanting others to think we're a successful believer, or have a successful ministry; the head and not the tail in every area of life. We've ignored or covered the true state of the soul. Many times we don't know others are

Yes, we can be anointed; but the bondages in our own souls keep us from truly connecting with one another in the body of Christ. We connect by words. We connect by doctrine. We even connect "in spirit." But rarely do we connect and stay connected with heart-to-heart relationships in the body of Christ. Toxic, destructive emotions prevent us from having our hearts to actually touch, to literally fasten together. They hinder us from experiencing a link and an emotional bond with one another through God's gift of love and pure, healed emotions. They blind us to reality. I don't believe the body of Christ will ever become one as long as there are shields and walls built by dysfunctional behavior and feelings in toxic proportions which block a pure and healthy flow of God-given emotions.

NO LOVE? NO REVIVAL

It's time for a change. It's time we learn how to relate to God and each other in an intimate, regular, healthy way. Then the world will know that we are one. That's part of *true* revival!

I met God in the most loving, compassionate, merciful, forgiving, and powerful way that I have ever experienced in my life and ministry. I found that it's okay to stand up in front of people and cry. I found that it's okay to become very close friends with others and gain trust back. It's okay to set healthy boundaries and abide by them, even if others violate them or misunderstand. It's okay to get away from unhealthy people who refuse to grow. It's okay to have problems and admit them. It's okay to feel emotions, express them properly, know what they are teaching you, and enjoy them!

Someone may say, "Well, people will think I don't have faith if I learn this emotional stuff."

Well, what do you think faith is for? Let people think what they want to think and you get the healing and understanding you need.

When you are attacked by the devil, he will take the advantage if you don't know the procedure for managing your emotions. There's a tremendous lack of teaching and revelation on this subject, not only in the body of Christ, but also in our nation. In case you haven't noticed, we are a culture that produces people who are becoming more and more emotionally unstable.

God wants to bring this understanding and revelation to every level of society. I believe the Spirit of the Lord is breaking the spirit of dysfunction – emotional and mental dysfunction in the body of Christ. The enemy attaches to dysfunction, and shames the people into hiding inside the church. He wants to keep us isolated, unable to function in normal everyday emotional healthy habits with God, with each other, and the world.

There are different timings for each of us, and God will work in the right timing for you. He always leads the right people to our paths to help us when we need help. I believe that is one reason you are reading this book right now.

I see a new day coming for the church. I see authentic people blending with a real living God, learning to love others where they are, and showing a genuine care and concern for their well-being.

When you are able to love yourself, heal your own emotional wounds – which we all battle at times – you will find out who you really are. Then you can love others and thrive in all areas of life. It is that love which the world will receive from the people of God, and it will usher in the great harvest of souls.

I want you to read on, and take steps in this journey with me. I believe you are in the timing that God has set for you, and that He is planting seeds for the total healing of your soul. You don't have to give up. There is hope for you; there are answers, and God is about to help you in a powerful way.

You are about to unlock your true identity!

Chapter 4

GOD WANTS YOU WELL
AT EVERY LEVEL

"*B*eloved, I wish above all things that thou mayest prosper and be in health, even as thy soul prospereth.*"*

3 John 2

I want you to notice that the Word says here, "in *all* things, and *be in health.*" I think we could probably paraphrase it to say, "Be in all health, or be *healthy in everything* – be *whole* in your spirit, soul, and body."

It's very clear from the Word of God that He has created us as a three-fold being. We are a spirit, we are born-again, and our spirit man is alive unto God. We have a soul, and we live in a body.

The recreated spirit of man is always well, because that's where God lives in the Christian. But we know that the soul and the body can become ill. It's not a shame for a Christian to say so when you are sick in your body. It's not showing a lack of faith if you have a problem! All it means is that you have the wonderful opportunity to apply the Word of God and pray about your situation. If you let Him, God will bring you the healing however He wants to.

It's also not a shame if you have an emotional or mental problem in your life. Again, the soul man is made up of the mind, the will, and the emotions. People can have sickness or weakness in their bodies, even Christians who love the Lord. There can be pain, numbness, or bondage in your emotional realm, just like you can also experience sickness or pain in your body.

In his book, <u>Healing for Damaged Emotions</u>, David Seamands explains, *"I believe that there is another realm of problems which requires a special kind of prayer and a deeper level of healing by the Spirit. Somewhere between our sins, on the one hand, and our sicknesses, on the other, lies an area the Scripture calls 'infirmities'."* [2]

He goes on to say that in the storage of our thoughts and emotions, there is a record: Memories are recorded and some are very alive. They directly and deeply affect our concepts, our feelings, and our relationships. They affect the way we look at life, at God, at others, and ourselves. Christians like you and me have confusing and contradicting behaviors. We are people with hurts, scars, and wrong learning that interferes with our present behavior.

Whatever part of your being is suffering, God wants you well and sound in that area.

DON'T GET NERVOUS!

In the church world, we get a little nervous when people talk about having mental or emotional difficulties. Usually we think of the extreme case, perhaps the people in the loony bins or the ones locked up in the psyche ward; but certainly not in the body of Christ. We also have a tendency to think that people just shouldn't have those problems, and definitely shouldn't bring them up, especially in public discussion. We also have a tendency to shun or judge people who are struggling with these "private issues."

I know there are simple, everyday Christians who love God, yet are suffering with these infirmities. Usually the problems don't qualify for the psyche ward. Nonetheless, there are still various and sometimes serious problems that stem from toxic emotions. If we are honest, we can all admit that we could grow, change, and learn more in this area. I needed to see a change if I was going to be healed, and if my personal relationships were going to function more effectively. Out of my adversity and my struggle, a victory was born.

Of those who struggle, some wrestle secretly, while others can't hide their pain or the emotional imbalance. Some accept their unhealthy thoughts and actions as normal; while others accept their behavior as part of their personality.

Most of us experience the effects of dysfunction because we live in a fallen world. In some way or another, or at some time or another in your life, you will need to know how to obtain and walk in emotional wellness.

So, if you can experience sickness and pain in your body, you certainly could experience a need for healing in your soul or your emotions! When we accepted Jesus Christ as our personal Savior and became born again, we didn't become redeemed or immuned from sickness. Instead, we were given access to the promises of God to receive the healing power of God into our situation whenever we needed it.

It's the same for the mind, the will, and the emotions. In many Christian circles, we're not used to the idea of allowing the healing power of God to flow into the emotional realm of our lives. For some reason, we've ignored and limited God in this area that He created.

HOW DID JESUS HANDLE IT?

When Jesus walked on the earth, do you think He ever left anything undone?

Think about the ten lepers in Luke 17. The very premise of that physical disease was tied to living with a daily overdose of shame. Everywhere a leper went, people would scatter. The leprous would have to announce their arrival by shouting, "Unclean! Unclean!" Talk about feeling rejected and bad about yourself!

When Jesus healed the lepers, do you think He stopped at the physical disease of it? No. I can just imagine how those lepers hurt inside, because they were rejected, outcasts of society. Every place they went, the lepers had to flaunt their sickness. And Jesus walked right up to them, healed their bodies *and* He healed their souls. He took the entire disgusting pain-filled package away from them, just like He took the whole thing away from me, and will take it away from you.

God wants you to be whole; spirit, soul, and body. He wants you to accept and receive His healing power into your emotional realm. I needed His healing power in my emotional realm. The Holy Spirit wanted to touch something there, and it changed my life in a very special and beautiful way.

"PROSPER" IS A LOADED WORD!

Let's read again our opening scripture.

"Beloved, I wish above all things that thou mayest prosper and be in health, even as thy soul prospereth."

The word "prosper" in this passage means *to thrive.* It doesn't isolate itself to monetary or financial areas only; it simply means to thrive with abundance in all areas of life.

Prosperity is not just in the financial realm. There are many Christians that can prosper financially; but when it comes to their soul life, or their spiritual life, they are not prospering or thriving as much as they can. We can prosper in one area and not in another, like relationships. We can have our prayer life to become strong, yet still not know how to manage our anger. That's why some can be spiritually mature yet soulishly immature. If a leader is spiritually mature yet soulishly immature, that ministry will be dysfunctional in several areas, and will eventually become dangerous if not healed.

"Prosper in all things." That means that God's prosperity, the flourishing nature of God, the loving nature of God, the intimacy and closeness of His being, wants to touch every area of your life – your spirit *and* your soul! God wants you to be like a flourishing plant.

YOU'LL GO AS FAR AS YOU'RE HEALED

I want you to also notice from 3 John 2 that the writer specifically points out that our **soul** must prosper or thrive. It's vitally important that your soul prosper and be in health, **because you can only go as far as your soul thrives.**

Many of us carry wounds and memories from our past, and the effects of those explains the reactions of our souls. Just because we are born-again doesn't mean that all of our problems have vanished. When you got saved, your hair color didn't change, you didn't grow more hair, and you didn't lose weight right away. Many of the problems and their effects were solved when you found the love of God. But most of those things you had to walk out patiently, applying discipline and the Word of God.

It's the same principle with some of the conditioning and experiences from our family life, or our background, or from things that have influenced our mental and emotional development. It takes understanding and time to walk out your healing process. God wants to powerfully move in those areas of your life and make you whole.

On that point, it is clear that we have an enemy of our soul, whose mission is to keep us from thriving and flourishing. The enemy of our soul is called **shame**.

Later, we will explore how shame as a toxic emotion cripples our lives and becomes devastating to us. You'll discover that one of the main attributes of shame is that it **hides**. For that reason, most of us don't even realize if we have shame in our lives because it is so hidden by the many masks we wear to cover "something we don't like" about ourselves. Experts in the emotional sciences agree that shame is one emotion that when it becomes toxic, affects other emotions as well. When shame is healed, the others can be tamed.

This book is going to have several phases as we explore the soul and the workings of toxic emotions; mainly acquired shame. First, I am laying a foundation for you to build upon. Some of you reading this book thought, like the old gospel songs, that the soul was the only portion that became born-again. Some have no idea that the soul is an entity in itself and has many facets.

TRUST GOD – YOU'RE SAFE!

If the things I say minister to you, then receive it and act upon it, and enjoy what God will do for you. It if doesn't, then throw out what you don't need and retain the rest. God may have led some of you to read this book just to know more about the subject of the soul, or more specifically, the emotional realm. Or, maybe you want to help a needy family member or friend. Others are on the verge of a nervous breakdown, totally disillusioned with the circumstances of life and have little idea why.

If you fit into any of the above categories, this book is for you. It is my mission and mandate from God to expose the devastating manifestations of toxic emotions – mainly focusing the study on toxic shame so that your life can be lived to its fullest, in its wholeness. Without knowledge, we perish. God is going to help you through as I give you some knowledge to help you work with some of the things affecting your life.

So I ask you to open up your heart, not to excuse your innermost feelings, and not to put off your healing because you think you're an extreme case. Please be open even if you don't think you need help in this area. God may surprise you like He did me! Let the Holy Spirit speak to you about what goes on in the deepest part of your life, or things that have happened in your life that He wants to minister healing to you. He also wants to discipline and train parts of your soul that are unmanageable for you right now. Just like He wants to heal your physical body, He wants to heal your heart and set you free.

As you read on, know this: **It is God's will** for you to prosper in your soul – your mind, will, and most definitely, your emotions.

Chapter 5

THE HEART OF GOD TOWARD PERSONAL WHOLENESS

"A bruised reed He will not break..."

Isaiah 42:3

Isn't that great about God? He takes you where you are and loves you and heals you. We've all had painful situations; situations where we were bruised on the inside. He doesn't break us; He heals us, and that's a beautiful promise.

We've touched on this already, but before we go further in the subject of this book, I want you to deeply understand the heart of God towards you. Whatever your emotional state, you are safe, free from any danger, harm, or further breaking with Him. Let's look more closely into His character.

"I will not bring any of the diseases I brought upon the Egyptians upon you, for I am the Lord who heals you."

Exodus 15:26

The Hebrew word for "heals" is *rophe*. God was saying, "I am Jehovah-Rophe." This Hebrew word is very interesting because it means to stitch or to mend. When the Lord is speaking of Himself here, He's not saying that He will only heal you of physical diseases. The very definition of the word implies that He's talking about brokenness – emotional and mental brokenness. God wants to stitch you back together, to mend the areas of your heart that have been ripped by life's trying and difficult circumstances, and by unhealthy people whose behavior influenced your development.

Look at it much like mending a torn cloth and stitching it back into its right condition.

There are specific incidents in our lives that can cause us to get our emotion, or soul off center. Jehovah Rophe knows how to get you back to functioning properly, the way He made you, and how to help your soul regain soundness and stability.

It is imperative before we delve any further into emotional healing, that you are firm and secure about who God is, and that He is completely and totally with you in this process. I want you to understand that this ability to mend is one of God's redemptive characteristics! It is a part of His being to repair the human soul and make it like new. He's not just interested in healing the outer person; He wants to heal the inner person; the part of you that makes you who you really are.

"I have satiated the weary soul and I have replenished every sorrowful soul."

Jeremiah 31:25

You will never find a case where the heart of God turns away from the multitudes who need healing and restoration in the emotional realm, or *any* realm for that matter. Throughout the Scriptures, men and women of God prayed to be healed in their inward parts, asking God to heal their broken, torn lives and put them back together. God never turned anyone away. He is always reaching out to us, building our hope and faith, so we can recognize and partake of His grace to heal in the area of emotional wholeness.

HE LOVES YOU WHERE YOU ARE

One of the greatest keys to developing intimacy with the Lord, is to recognize and accept that He loves you right where you are – no matter what has happened to you or how it has happened He doesn't care how badly you are hurting or what you have done or haven't done. He is a loving, gentle God who is there, *now*, for you.

That fact can be understood through the experience of salvation. It's amazing how quickly we can forget about God's love, acceptance, and grace after we've matured in the Lord. Our walk is still draped with His grace and His mercy. God doesn't love you or do more for you because you've preached all over the world, or because you have a ministry or a position in the church. He loves you unconditionally because you are His child. Of course there are times when God rebukes you and corrects you as well. But because healing shame is a very delicate operation, we will focus on the deep love and compassionate understanding of our God.

Many times I've heard people say, "I'm fighting depression, unforgiveness, or whatever – *but* I'm working in the church." No, my friend – don't miss the key!

Your Heavenly Father wants to tell you that His love never fails, and because of that, you can throw yourself over on Him completely. He wants to teach you about His compassion and His tenderness. He wants to show you how non-judgmental He really is. He is full of grace. He wants you free from PERFORMANCE MENTALITY.

Some Christians have based their entire relationship with God (and others) on a performance orientation instead of the simple, accepting, warm grace of God. You don't have to earn your emotional healing; you just have to receive it. These precious and tender, sometimes tough issues, only God can completely heal, no matter *what* you do.

REMEMBER THE WOMAN AT THE WELL?

Let's read the story of the woman at the well in John 4. Later, you can read it for yourself verse by verse; but I want to tell it as a story. It represents how safe we are with the Lord, and that He meets us right where we are.

Being a Samaritan, right away she was a reject. The Jews in Jerusalem discriminated against Samaria because they felt the Samaritans desecrated the true worship of Jehovah. The Samaritans took some of the Jewish customs and incorporated their own beliefs with it, and the Jews felt the Samaritans were unclean because of it. In fact, Jewish disgust was so great, in their travels they would go completely around the area of Samaria to get to their destination, even if it meant a weeks worth of extra traveling. They wanted nothing to do with the country or the people.

But here was Jesus going through Samaria instead of around it, because He is a man of love. Maybe He was also a bit curious about how the people there were really doing! He sits down at a place called Jacob's Well because He was tired and thirsty. A Samaritan woman approached the well and Jesus said to her, "Give me a drink."

You know that Jesus knew all about this woman. Not only was she a Samaritan, but she had been married five times and now was living with a man. In this day and age, someone might have said to her, "I see you have failure problems in your relationships..."

But Jesus saw the potential in her. He said, "Will you give me something to drink?" Why did He ask her that? Because He was going after her heart.

This is who Jesus really is. He talked to her, reached out to her, and was kind to her. His attitude must have portrayed that He really cared about her, and that He was interested in who she was as a person. I pray that God restores to the church the art of talking to one another with tenderness, interest, and care. The more you do your emotional work, it will happen. You will open up, and so will the people around you because they will sense and see that you are a safe person.

Jesus was preparing the ground for a miracle. Notice that He was by Himself. The disciples were gone. Sometimes you've got to get the super-spiritual folks away so that a true heart miracle can happen!

The woman began to open up to Him. Why? Because she sensed He was safe and supportive; and it was her appointed time to be healed of the shame in her life. She questioned Him, "Hey, how can you as a Jew, ask me for something to drink?"

Jesus just replied, "If you knew the gift of God, you would have asked Him for living water; but you didn't know." He's carefully working on her heart, taking the time to prepare a safe environment for her, getting her to open up to Him. He keeps asking for something to drink.

Finally, she blurts out, "Hey, hey, HEY! Whatever you're talking about – something that I don't have, you've got. There's something about you..."

It wasn't just the anointing this woman noticed. It was God; it was the presence of wholeness that she so desired. She wanted pure love. She was a broken woman who needed healing. As they continued to relate in the warm, safe environment Jesus created, she asked, "Can you give me living water?"

When Jesus saw that her heart was opened, He said, "Go call your husband."

He had created such an atmosphere of honesty and trust, that He knew He could ask her that leading question so He could help her. Jesus knew she now trusted Him enough to be honest; even in knowing He was a Jew!

"I don't have a husband."

The woman answered honestly because she knew He wasn't going to rebuke her and say, "Curse you woman! You don't have any faith! You aren't living by our standards!"

Jesus didn't do any of that. He just answered, "No, I know he's not your husband. You've had five, and the one you're with now is not a husband either."

Allow me to paraphrase further. Jesus answered this woman and said, "I know all that, and guess what? **I still love you. I love you anyway. I love you in the middle of your mess.**" There was no pretending, because at that moment, this Samaritan woman was looking right into the face of God.

UNCONDITIONAL LOVE IS SPELLED: G-O-D

Do you know what Jesus was doing? What He does best. I can just see His eyes sparkling with love, mercy, forgiveness, and grace. I'm sure He was smiling at her, calming her every fear. He was getting ready to change her life forever. She had vulnerably revealed her heart to Him in a safe environment, and now He was there to comfort her while the transformation took place. Isn't that wonderful?

It doesn't matter what has happened in your life. God knows it all and He still loves you. You are safe with Him. It's safe to tell Him and the trusted confidants that God has placed in your life. Tell the truth about all the problems and the thoughts deep in your heart. Tell the whole story. Don't hide or forget anything. Now is the time to talk. Now is the time where what's in your heart needs to come out, so you can bring it into the light and heal it.

God wants an intimate relationship with every part of your life; and He will be there for you when it seems too hard or painful to tell. But, you must let Him work deep inside of you. He will help you open up when it's easier to hide, lie, or deny that there are issues inside that have affected your emotions, your very way of life.

Your God will also give you someone to listen to you, hug you, and empathize with the pain of the shame you could uncover on your journey into health. Someone will also be there to encourage you to get out of it as well.

You don't have to live with that mess any longer. How could we ever change if we didn't know that Jesus absolutely and unconditionally loves us right where we are?

Chapter 6

THE WORLD OF EMOTIONS

We criticize them, make fun of them, act like we don't have them, or ignore them. But do we really know what emotions are? Do we know what they are designed by God to do in our lives and through our lives?

Not long ago, I had an officer from the Bloomington Police Department come and speak at our church. A segment of our ministry reaches out to families of the community with seminars that teach awareness and protection for children in victimization and safety issues, which I call the "Family Awareness Project."

I asked this officer to tell us the number one problem they had in the area. I couldn't believe what I heard. Do you know what it was? Road rage!

He didn't say murder, burglaries, domestic violence, drug dealers, prostitution, or gangs. He said road rage!

In our nation as a whole, Christian and secular, we are hurting emotionally. We have people that are so cold and hardened in their hearts, that they don't even need to take drugs or be drunk to kill someone else. Road rage is just another example. It's the result of bottled up emotions that go into a rampage when an unknown person touches that area of the soul.

God is wanting to heal us in the very deepest part of our being.

One of the reasons that we detach from our emotions is because we are afraid to talk about them. We don't know what they are and what they're supposed to do. We are simply uneducated on this topic. We as Christians think we should focus only on the spiritual side of life. But God is a God of complete wholeness in every area of life, including emotional wholeness.

Some of the painful situations and incidents that evolve in the body of Christ are because people are not well emotionally, or they have not healed areas of their lives that are dysfunctional. Many have insecurities, emotional weaknesses, emotions out of control, or emotions that they've numbed. These emotional issues can cause spiritual, physical, and relational problems.

THE ROOT SYSTEM

I want to define what I mean by the word "issues," because I plan to continue to use that expression throughout this book.

What I'm really referring to is more of a concept and an expression than anything else. Issues in someone's life speaks of a package that the person presents about themselves. This undesirable package is made up of both the *inner source* of an individual's problems, combined with the *visible evidence* and effects, or manifestation of the problem.

Another way to illustrate this would be to look at the roots and fruits of a plant as an example. An issue begins with the intricate root system of the problem. There can be more than one *root* in the system – toxic emotions, generational curses, personality, demonic influences, and so on. Together with the *fruit* – visible results, behavior, actions, reactions, habits, lifestyles, et cetera – create a reality which I call an **issue**.

In this book, I will be focusing primarily on the emotional part of the root system and the emotional results which I call emotional issues. Issues may be varied, overlap, and may be mental, spiritual, physical or will-based, depending upon the individual. Whatever the case, they are considered unhealthy.

Another way to describe this would be any conflict, concern or potential problem, whether conscious or unconscious, that is incomplete for us or needs action or change. When these difficulties begin to be deeply examined, they usually don't present themselves as an issue, rather they present themselves first as simple problems in every day life. After some persistent examination and description of the feelings surrounding the problem, it can become clear which issue or issues are involved.

Experts in this field classify the primary core emotional issues as: control, trust, feelings, being overly responsible, neglecting our own needs, all-or-none thinking and behaving, high tolerance for inappropriate behavior, low self-esteem, being real, grieving our ungrieved losses, fear of abandonment, difficulty resolving conflict and difficulty giving and receiving love.

DISTORTED TEACHING BREEDS FEAR

In the body of Christ, we're strong spiritually, we're getting renewed in our minds, but we're weak emotionally and because of that, we're immature and sometimes unstable. Emotional issues are surfacing.

Maybe one reason we've been afraid to explore the emotional realm is because many people have been led around by their emotions in the past. A lot of times, people make their decisions and base their lives totally and com-pletely on how they feel. God doesn't want it to be that way.

Until we get our emotions in the right order with some knowledge and some ministry, you and I will continue to make emotionally-based decisions on feelings alone.

I must say that we've gone overboard to some degree. We've been taught that we can't be led by how we feel. I *can't be led* by how I feel, but I have to acknowledge how I feel because that is a part of me! I *can't deny* how I feel; I must understand how I feel and why I feel that way, but I don't have to be led by it or make my decisions by the feelings.

God gave us our feelings. He gave us our emotions; but sometimes in the church we're afraid to express emotion. We think it's spiritual to be under control and to look like we have everything all together. If someone cries, we get nervous. We want someone to give them a tissue or have the usher escort them out of the room!

If you mention things about emotions to Christian believers, there are different reactions, the primary being wariness. Why? Because often we don't understand them, we don't know what they are, and we haven't understood the place they have in our spiritual lives.

For example, if someone is depressed or has some other emotional need, some resort to a critical, judgmental mode, saying things like, "Well, it must be a punishment from God. He/she must not be a tither and is under a curse. He/she must be in rebellion to authority." Or, "If you seek help in that area, you are doubting God's ability to heal you." Some even think the problems are deserved!

It's true that people do get a little weird when their emotions are not working correctly. That's why they need someone to help them, someone who understands what emotions are and what they're designed by God to do. Then, after healing, it's not weird to express healthy emotions.

We're not used to being vulnerable with one another or before one another. Yet the New Testament is full of descriptions where Paul says, "Be tenderhearted, merciful, compassionate, empathic, and understanding towards one another." That means that when you're in pain, I shouldn't be afraid of it or try to ultimately suppress, belittle, or minimize your need for emotional expression. I should be free enough to feel your pain or your joy, to empathize with you, and help you through it.

GOD IS THE AUTHOR OF EMOTIONS

Allow me to make two very powerful statements. **If you're out of contact with your emotions, you're out of contact with life. In fact, if you're ignoring your emotions, stifling them in yourself and in everyone else, you're out of contact with God.**

I want you to see the personality of God as a true illustration of what emotions are. God is an emotional God. Yes, you read that correctly. In fact, emotions all started with God!

God cries, He laughs, He's full of joy, He is saddened, He's grieved, and He gets angry. Of course, we're cautious to say that He gets angry, because it's so strongly taught that God is a good God – and He is! But sometimes He gets angry.

Here's the difference with the way we understand His emotions versus ours. God knows there is nothing wrong with getting upset, because He knows how to manage anger appropriately. God doesn't knock you around when He gets angry. He doesn't verbally abuse you when He's upset. His anger only lasts for a moment. He has taught us through the Word that it's okay to feel anger; just know how to handle it – don't let the sun go down without resolving it, and do not sin with it.

Understand that emotions are given by God to you. You are to feel a full range of emotions, depending upon what circumstances you are in. **These emotions should then teach you something; then proceed through you (run their full course), properly connecting you to yourself, to people, situations, and to God, helping you live a whole-some life.** They are not supposed to become like strangers living in your house; they're not supposed to build a camp-fire on the inside of you, forcing you to become trapped or fastened in a certain feeling. No, **you are supposed to participate with your emotions.** God gave you emotions to make contact with life, with people, and with Him.

Before we go any further, let's study a variety of healthy, emotional responses so that we can see what they look like individually, and then how they become toxic when shame distorts them. I believe we must first understand how emotions are supposed to operate through our lives before we can understand how they become toxic.

Chapter 7

HEALTHY EMOTIONS

E motions are a basic, powerful, soulish function that have been given by God to every human being. Very simply, they are the part of our consciousness that involve feelings. Emotions are universal to every person, which all of us, both man and woman, need to learn more about.

There is a clear understanding you must have about emotions to help you stay stable and sound in them. One of the keys to emotional health is maintaining a proper balance of each emotion and between different emotions.

Any emotion in your life can be used in one of two ways: either to *rule* your life or to *teach* you about life. We should experience emotions; but the emotions shouldn't be like an unwanted guest that comes to your house, makes a fire in your fireplace, settles in, and lives there subjecting your entire outlook on life to its influence. When an emotion or feeling makes a home in us and doesn't move, it can become built up. High levels of unprocessed emotions can become toxic. Allowing excess emotions to rule or dominate is dangerous because, although they are powerful, they are very unreliable.

Healthy emotions are feelings that pass through our emotional channels in a normal way. These channels allow us to feel the feeling, to be taught something by it, and then move on. If we don't allow an emotion to follow its God-given procedure, we can become "stuck" in it. Then unconsciously we allow that emotion or feeling to distort many aspects of our inner life. We can begin to misinterpret the actions of others, or fall victim to negative personal traits and thoughts. The cycle can be repeated over and over. We don't know what to do with these intense feelings, so we try to "stuff" them or we lose emotional control. Then we try to hide the fruit or seek other solutions to what this issue is producing instead of simply doing some emotional work, to heal the emotional system at the roots.

ACCEPT RESPONSIBILITY

I want to stress that having a dangerous emotional build-up is not an *excuse* for anyone to continue in sin or unhealthy behaviors, which are the fruits of toxic emotions. By your very study of this book, you are taking a step to accept your responsibility. Whether you were sinned against, or you are controlled by an addiction, you must take action *to heal* and then to change. Healing toxic emotions is sometimes the very key to a change in behaviors and habits. Still, some people will use every excuse possible to take the light off what the Spirit of God is gently confronting about the issues in their lives. Do not resist God and say your problem is because of bad emotions and stop there. If you do, you'll never be free to walk in the wholeness God has provided. This book has keys that will help you do some of your own emotional work.

Remember, emotions are a tool given to you so that you can monitor your basic human necessities. They help you regulate your need for support, loss, encouragement, et cetera; without them we would be unaware of our most basic, fundamental needs. That's why people who deny their emotions or completely suppress them walk around like a spiritual robot, eventually crumbling under the weight of their own neediness.

The real self is to experience all of our emotions in the right way, the right time, and in moderation for the right situation. It's when we get stuck inside of an emotion that we need to have the Holy Spirit to bring revelation so that we can be healed.

ENERGY IN MOTION

Emotions are not your enemies. I like to say it like this: they are "e-motion," or energy in motion. They are a fuel to help you act to meet all your needs in a healthy way. Then you can live a satisfied, fulfilled, and wholesome life.

Because they are so important, you're supposed to feel them! They are designed to teach you about yourself, about others, about God, and situations. When they are felt in a proper way, they help you to live a normal life (by God's standards) the way He intended for you to live. And yes, although as believers we are a peculiar people, set apart by God, and citizens of heaven, we must learn to live a healthy life while on earth so that we can be a true witness of Jesus Christ.

Being aware of your emotions or having some emotional intelligence gives us several advantages in life. Emotions both warn us and assure us. They act as indicators or gauges of how we are doing at that moment or over a stretch of time. Our emotions give us a sense of being alive and of mastery. Emotions send us messages that something important may be happening, or that something might need our attention. We must listen to them.

A SPECTRUM OF FEELINGS

Let's explore some of these "e-motions," this energy given by God. This is not an all decisive list. You might be surprised at what you read, because most of the following basic emotions are usually classified as "negative emotions" that must be suppressed. That is because they are often uncomfortable to feel. But, **God doesn't have classifications with emotions. He has purpose with emotions.** To Him, there are no positive or negative emotions. There are no labels. With God, it's simply a full spectrum of emotions. They are all given for a specific function. We are the ones who label them as good or bad because of the way we experience them.

GRIEF

Grief is what most of us would classify as a negative emotion, because when we feel it, it's a sensation that is very uncomfortable, sometimes sad. But grief is an important emotion given to us by God, with the purpose of processing and handling loss.

We all experience loss. It is part of normal life. Think of the times when you have been unable to maintain, sustain, or keep something that was very precious to you. Perhaps it was a loved one, a pet, a job, a church, a friend, or a dream. To be deprived of someone or something that met a very special need in our lives, or to go without something that we had and valued, something that we needed, wanted, or expected, can affect us – either slightly where we can easily get over it, or very traumatically.

Second Corinthians 7:10 tells us to grieve, but not to grieve by the sorrow of the world. There is a godly way to grieve particular situations. When we have sinned, we should grieve the mistake and separation from God; then repent. When there is loss which evokes emotional pain, we need to grieve over the loss, allow the grieving mechanism have its full course; then move on.

To sorrow after the way of the world means that healthy grief is turned into a continuing, constant, unending mourning. The sorrow of the world causes the griever to be *fixed* on themselves and the grief, pain, and hopelessness he/she feels instead of letting go. There is no hope; no way to recover from a continual feeling of pain. Despondency and depression sets in, and it can turn into a real, emotional mess.

We're not supposed to become fixed upon or to have an emotion become embedded in our being. When I say grieve, I mean to allow yourself to actually feel the shock, anxiety, anger, pain, and despair (not all at once, please). They are all parts of the grieving process, and each person will experience it differently. That's why God's Word says to let it happen. With God's way, there is hope. I may repeat myself several times, but I want to arm you with continual knowledge. So when we get stuck (fixed, blocked) in any emotion, positive or negative, problems can abound.

We really haven't learned how to process loss. We teach our little boys not to cry because we want everyone to see that they are a man, and they are strong. Some Christians believe that if you cry at a funeral, then you're not showing the hope we have in God. We teach to be either numb or excessive. What we're actually advocating is emotional bondage, because everyone needs to grieve and to include tears if that's how you feel. It has nothing to do with being strong, but it has everything to do with being a human being and living with a proper emotional response in your life. God created us to be a supernatural human being, but to grieve over loss, to meet the need you have as you experience pain; then to process it and move ahead.

This is a natural process that God has given all people to go through. This process has in itself the power to heal.

I've lost a few relationships in my life that were painful for me. Not just romantic relationships, but friendships as well, where the enemy came in and ripped me off. Loss can be very painful. The loss of a job, the loss of a loved one in death, or the loss of a marriage.

IS *EVERYTHING* SPIRITUAL?

Jesus, who is our example, wasn't bound up in His emotions. When He went to the tomb of Lazarus, He was touched by the pain of losing a friend. He needed to process His grief and He wept there.

"Oh, Mary Alice, Jesus wept because of the spiritual unbelief of the people there."

We're really setting ourselves up for danger and defeat when we believe that everything is a spirit. It's lop-sided Christianity to think that way. If everything was spiritual, then what are we doing with a body? I know many Christians that have grief trapped somewhere inside of their being, and it affects them. They know how to fight in the spirit; but they're hurting on the inside and can't figure out how to get the full victory. Over and over, at different times they are feeling grief. That grief affects their attitudes, decisions, et cetera. When the feeling leaves, they are okay. Sometimes they don't know they are feeling what they are feeling; so they don't know what to do with it. Obviously, they never learned how to process the emotional part of their battle. They know how to spiritually heal; but not emotionally. They know how to spiritually refill; but not emotionally.

I believe in spiritual influences. For example, there is a spirit of rejection; but not everything is a spirit. I've dealt with the spirit of fear; but you still have to manage the feeling of fear in your soul that is sometimes left over from the spiritual activity or the circumstance.

If we blame every emotion on a spirit, such as the spirit of joy, the spirit of depression, the spirit of fear, then we're going to blame the enemy for everything and miss our make-up as human beings. What a maturing thing for the body of Christ, to live not only in spiritual power; not only in divine health for our physical bodies; but to mature and become skillful in managing our emotions as well. **I believe in and practice deliverance from evil forces, but I am also learning emotional intelligence.**

No, Jesus wept because He *felt* the pain of those He dearly loved. He wasn't an emotional basket-case. He knew how to feel emotion, how to express emotion, and why He was doing it. Aren't you glad that today, He is still touched by the *feeling* of your infirmities (Hebrews 4:15)?

Emotional pain is something we don't like to experience, but we must. Some people are so numb they can't or won't follow through to feel pain at all. Pain tells you something; it's supposed to signal that something is wrong and must be handled. Some people walk around like a zombie, trying to medicate their emotional pain instead of allowing it to have its full course. If you need to manage your emotional pain through medication, I'm not criticizing it. But make sure you are seeking an answer to gain a complete recovery and you're not trying to subdue it, medicating it so you can pretend it's not there.

Understand that in the midst of a negative world, God has given us an emotional release that produces wholeness in our lives. Grief is one of those emotions.

ANGER

I always thought that as a Christian woman, you should never become angry – especially if you are a minister of the gospel. I had the subtle fear that if I properly expressed any type of anger, people would really misjudge me, criticize me, call me a Jezebel, or even be turned away from God.

You might be saying, "Well, if I show anger, then how can I praise the Lord, be joyful in every situation, and have faith?"

You should praise the Lord. But you should also be honest and not afraid to acknowledge how you really feel. "Hey, that really ticked me off," is not a bad confession, it's just the truth. And you don't have to act on it. You can feel it and control it. You can also express it in the proper way, with the proper people.

If you don't process anger correctly, it will build inside of you; and I promise it will come out one way or another. Eventually, excess anger shows itself passively or aggressively, when you least want it to come out. Someone will certainly "push your buttons" or find a way to get to you. The need to express anger is a part of human nature, and a given in the dynamics of human relationships.

Specialists tell us that if we suppress anger, it can become depression. Sometimes physical diseases come from anger that's been stuffed. If you're a minister and you've suppressed anger instead of processing it properly, your sermon messages can sound bitter, sharp, and hard. The congregation will leave feeling beat-up instead of encouraged. You may not even be aware of how your anger is affecting them if you are not in touch with this powerful emotion.

Anger is an emotion given by God, to show you that **you've been violated**. The Lord said we could be angry, but we shouldn't sin. We should acknowledge the anger and the accompanying feeling before the sun sets.

There are many Christians who don't know what to do with this naturally occurring emotion named anger. They don't even know that their anger directs their lives. They're so full of anger that they can easily carry offense. Or, they have so little feeling of anger, they allow themselves to be constantly violated by others.

Revenge, wrath, bitterness, offense, criticism, judgment can be rooted in toxic anger. There is a real emotion that you feel when violated; and if you are violated enough times, or by someone who is very precious to you and you don't know it's there or what to do with it, the devil can attach to it and create all kinds of havoc. Anger out of control can become sin. It can produce results that can cause you to be very sorry that you didn't heal it. Unprocessed anger, whether it is stuffed or expressed, can destroy individuals and relationships.

Remember, God gets angry; but it's only for a moment. He allows Himself to feel anger, and He expresses the fact that He's been violated. You can read in the New Testament where Jesus went into the temple one day and knocked the tables over. He wasn't in a rage, but He was honest and righteously demonstrative about how He felt.

It's easy to be afraid to express anger, because we've all experienced people who have attacked us with their negative emotions, or darkness. that is not a fun experience, yet we learn that anger can create intense pain and damage if it is mismanaged. If you've been hurt by someone else's toxic emotions, God wants to heal you of that as well.

When anger is expressed within its proper boundaries, it becomes a positive fuel that gives us the strength and energy we need to make correct choices and glean important facts about situations in our lives.

SADNESS

Sadness is also an uncomfortable emotion. None of us really like experiencing it. It was very hard to turn on the television and watch the sadness of the Littleton, Colorado community after it's children killed other children not long ago.

Do you know what I found out when God began to heal my toxic emotions and teach me emotional soundness? After I healed some of the unprocessed sadness in my heart, it was much easier to be empathic with others. I could identify and really understand how they felt, because I had allowed myself to establish healthy habits concerning sadness – both my own feelings and the feelings of others. I was able to be like Jesus and be far more compassionate than I've ever been in my whole life!

I wept as I watched those people in that community go through their pain and suffering. I felt for them. I allowed myself to be like Jesus, and to be touched with the feeling of their infirmity. I wasn't able to do that as easily before, because I was unknowingly bound up in my own emotions. My mindset was wrong. I knew we had to acknowledge things, but I thought I had to be tough. I thought sentimentality was a little weak. As with others, I had to be a "warrior" for God. I was wrong.

Sadness actually releases emotional energy to heal our pain. If we hold sadness inside, it freezes the pain within us.

FEAR

The emotional intelligence concerning fear is that it warns us of danger. Fear tells me that my basic needs aren't going to be met in a situation. And because of that, it causes me to hesitate or be paralyzed.

As infants, it's said that only two things challenged those basic needs: the fear of loud noise and the fear of being dropped!

Positive, healthy fear is an emotion leading to discernment and wisdom. Don't you agree with me that sometimes people need more healthy fear? Sometimes kids – and adults – act fearless in a stupid way, acting a little on the crazy side. Fear can be an intuition that keeps you and your loved ones protected.

Although the God-kind of fear and a self-preserving fear is good, fear can also be negative and out of balance. Fear has three basic areas of its negativity. Fear areas can come from circumstances that you have *known*; from the unexpected occurrences that *might happen*; and from an unrealistic paranoia that *will never happen*. Unhealthy fear can put such a grasp on your life that it can smother your true identity. As an emotion, if unhealthy fear becomes stuck inside of you, it destroys your best self, damages your relationships, and paralyzes every decision in your life.

JOY

Joy is an exhilarating energy. So is compassion, hope, enthusiasm, and contentment. Like the feeling of love, joy is a great emotion, isn't it? Both of these emotions are wonderful feelings that tell us when all of our needs are being met. It's one we like to have around a lot. We want to sing, run, and jump when we have joy. When we feel this way, everyone we meet is a friend. The sky is bluer and the birds sing happier. When we feel love or joy, it signals to us that all is well.

Even though it's a greatly desired emotion, have you ever seen someone fixed in the emotion of joy? They can drive you crazy with their over-happy hyperness about everything and their fixed, plastic smile! At times these types of people seem so phony. I don't know about you, but sometimes I just feel a little bit like I might want to shake them to help them get unstuck! But as a whole, joyful feelings make us feel a sense of strength, well-being, and completion. Unconditional love produces bliss, compassion, empathy, enthusiasm, and contentment.

GUILT

Guilt can be a healthy emotion because it lets us know when we have violated values, morals, or boundaries. When we *do* something wrong, guilt is the emotion we feel that tells us we need to go back and fix it. Guilt is an emotion that speaks to you about your actions or behavior. Guilt is not to be confused with shame.

The emotion of guilt is our conscience-former. Unlike the shame we are going to discuss, guilt is exonerated when we, in our own strength, go back and change a situation that we were responsible for.

Let's use the game of football as an analogy. Shame is a violation of the game itself, a failure to obtain a goal, like never reaching the end zone. Guilt is just a violation of a rule, a behavioral penalty like being off sides, holding, or clipping. Shame deals with the inner core of the being; guilt deals more with the action. Shame makes you feel that you *are* the problem; guilt is the feeling that your *actions* caused a problem.

SHAME

There is a healthy shame. Shame is also a basic emotion that God has given. It is an identity emotion. Shame speaks to us our limits as human beings; it calls us to humility and to our need for God. It warns us not to try to be more or less human than we are. It gives us permission to be human. Healthy shame leads us to repentance. A sinner feels shame before God, and that's a good thing to feel. If you have sinned and it has separated you from God, then shame causes you to return to Him. It is an emotion that brings us to the altar saying, "There's a God; I'm a sinner and I need Him." That power was God; and the emotion of shame, the feeling of being a bad person, was used to bring us to a place of humility.

So a positive amount of healthy shame places us in a temporary state, telling us something is seriously wrong in our relationship with the world or our families. In a higher sense, healthy shame tells us something is wrong with our relationship with God.

Healthy shame reinforces the principle of humility. No person is intrinsically better or worse than anyone else. It's good to know that we are limited, in that we have very little control over the behavior of others, but that we can control our own actions.

Healthy shame is an emotion that makes you feel small. It's supposed to. It's supposed to show you that you are not the king or queen of the earth, that there is someone over you, that there are consequences to your actions. So it's very healthy to have a good dose of the right kind of shame.

There's a healthy amount of shame that we developed when we were children. When a child gets corrected in the right way, it produces a healthy shame. If our correction is healthy, it keeps us grounded. The problem is, because of the lack of emotional healing or the lack of knowledge in parents, we sometimes got an overdose of shame. That's when shame becomes unhealthy and toxic.

People with no healthy shame are emotionally immature. They act like the center of attention; they're immodest and immoral. They exhibit a lack of discretion and tact.

Have you ever seen a shameless teenager or adult? Their behavior is filled with a lack of dignity and honor. If a shameless person is around you for very long, the person will take you down with them. In fact, shamelessness can destroy a nation.

We live in a time of shamelessness, where people will cross boundaries that many years ago, they would have never crossed. Boundaries are crossed on things that are private, that are pure, that are dignified, in every aspect of life. When exposed, it seems that no one feels shame for the tender dignity of life that God gave, when we should feel ashamed. In Jeremiah 8:12, we can read that when people are in sin and are shameless, they lose their ability to blush. Their heart is hardened and they can't recognize the tender and precious emotion of healthy shame.

PERSONAL BOUNDARIES ARE IMPORTANT

I want to interject an important concept at this point in our study. Boundaries are vital to understanding emotional health, because when boundaries are violated, depending on the degree and the frequency of the violation, they become a major factor in determining whether an emotion becomes toxic or not.

Pia Mellody, in her book, Facing Codependence, describes boundaries as *"systems that are invisible and* symbolic 'fences' that have three purposes: (1) to keep people from coming into our space and abusing us; (2) to keep us from going into the space of others and abusing them; (3) to give each of us a way to embody our sense of 'who we are'." [3]

Boundaries have external parts which allow us to choose our distance from other people, and enable us to give or refuse permission for them to touch us. The internal boundaries protect our thinking, feelings, and behavior. When we understand both internal and external boundaries, we can take responsibility for them and keep them **separate** from the boundaries of **others.**

Very small children have no boundaries; intact boundaries are to be learned at home. The author goes on to say, "People who have grown up in dysfunctional homes usually suffer from various kinds of boundary impairment, and are either not protected enough, or are too protected. Boundary impairment includes: (1) no boundaries; (2) damaged boundaries; (3) walls instead of boundaries; and (4) moving back and forth from walls to no boundaries." [4]

Boundaries distinguish us from others. They separate us and set us apart. When we heal our emotions, then it is easier to set good boundaries to help us determine what we are responsible for and what we are not responsible for in our lives and relationships.

There is very good material for study on this subject, which I mention at the back of the book. You will begin to understand more about how boundaries fit into the emotional wholeness picture, as I continue in the teaching and it all becomes clear to you.

As we resume our study of shame, you might be asking these questions. Why is the emotion of shame so important? Why do I focus on shame? **Because when shame is in its toxic form, a healthy emotion has changed to become the**

state of your being. In other words, **it takes over or transforms into an identity.**

Shamelessness, unhealthy shame, and toxic shame didn't enter the world through our generation. We weren't the first to fall into it's dark and despondent clutches. It started long before your parents and great-great-grandparents. Remember, the shame that is dangerous began in the garden.

These are examples of just a few of the feelings we all experience sometime in life. There are plenty of other god-given emotions that there is not room enough here to expound on. A healthy person is empowered with a wider range of possibilities than we might have ever believed. Being healthy emotionally allows us to be flexible and creative within so that we can "roll with the punches of life" and come up standing!

Now, I want to introduce you to a primary culprit to toxic emotions. The assignment of this enemy is to thwart your emotions, to distort them, causing you to disguise your true self. This foe deceives you into consistently responding to mostly painful, negative feelings, or to numbness, with no feelings at all. You may be surprised at what you will discover as you read on. The name of your deadliest enemy is, toxic shame.

Chapter 8

DANGER! SHAME AS A STATE OF BEING

"**F**or I am conscious of my transgressions and I acknowledge them; my sin is EVER before me."
Psalm 51:3, Amplified Version

Think about one of the most embarrassing moments in your life.

What kind of story would you tell? Right now as you think of it, you'll probably laugh; but at the time it happened, it wasn't very funny.

I think one of the most embarrassing moments of my life was when I was a student at Oral Roberts University. I found myself wanting to be popular, especially with the guys. This was sort of new to me, because when I was in high school, all I cared about was good grades and being a good athlete, so boys never mattered much. But now I was in college, and well, my outlook expanded.

I was from the northern part of the United States, and I noticed that all the southern girls dressed differently, acted differently, and to put it simply, they were cute. So I began to look at what made them different from me.

In those days, all the southern girls wore these little slide shoes with a strap in the front and a spiky heel that made you five to six inches taller than you really were. The shoes were called Candies. I noticed that every pretty girl wore these shoes.

I remember thinking, I'm going to buy a pair of those shoes. I phoned my mother to tell her what I was going to do. She was a bit hesitant with her reply. God had already blessed me with good height. I had played basketball all through high school, and in flat shoes, I was still taller than some of these girls in spikes! "Just be careful," she said. I noticed she was tense. I don't know whether she knew me or she knew something about the shoes!

I ran out and bought myself a pair of Candies. I was so excited. The shoes were very feminine and they were the latest style. I was looking good. But looking good is not what I remember most about that fateful day.

Coming out of my room, I cautiously tried out my new shoes at the top of the stairs. I was doing my best to try to keep them on and walk at the same time! One step at a time, I balanced the position of my foot and handled myself well. I felt confident and ready to step out into the world.

Once outside, I was standing at the top of the busiest dormitory stairway on the entire campus. Pretending I was a pro at walking in these shoes, I put my foot down on the first step.

Somehow, some ungodly way, my foot got caught in the safety tape on the step that was supposed to keep you from falling. The tape failed miserably. I caught the bottom of the heel with my other foot, and I not only started to fall – I tumbled and rolled – legs flying wildly – down one, two, three, four flights of steps! And as if the entire school body watching wasn't enough, I didn't stop at the bottom of the steps – I rolled into the ditch, with only the surrounding fence stopping my hideous nightmare of nightmares!

Of course, I was immediately taken by friends to the hospital to see if my leg was broken. I remember at the time not even caring about my leg. The worst thing I had to deal with was not the pain in my body – it was that it happened at eight o'clock in the morning and everyone on their way to class saw me! I was nursing a very bruised and embarrassed ego!

WHAT ARE YOU CONSTRUCTING?

I want you to imagine the most embarrassing moment that you could ever have. Then, allow yourself to feel the feeling of that moment. It's a very uncomfortable feeling, isn't it? It makes you want to hide and makes you feel pretty bad about yourself as a person. Now multiply that feeling over and over and over again. Imagine that feeling fixed on the inside of you, and never being able to get away from it. Even though it's usually unconscious, **that's how the** *common* **emotion of shame feels.** *Toxic* **shame is more than just a feeling; it is a tragic occurrence where shame becomes a state of being.**

Let me quickly interject that Jesus Christ has healed us of *spiritual shame*. We've learned that as believers, Christ has made us righteous, and we can stand boldly without fear, without intimidation, without inadequacy before a loving Father who receives us and accepts us. But many believers carry around excess emotional shame that still makes them feel inferior; not in their spiritual lives, but in their everyday mental and emotional lives. They can stand before the Father, but continually they wilt when they stand before man, even when they know spiritual truths.

Or, they conceal their shame through a constructed personality. What I mean by that is, usually the soul goes into operation to construct a larger-than-life personality to quiet the shaming voices. As Keith Miller says in his book, The Secret Life Of The Soul, because of the false self that is built, we begin to be dishonest with ourselves, others, and God. Because we are busy constructing this false personality, we also start to make the wrong personal relationship choices, live in grandiosity through constant over-commitment, construct self-fulfilling social relationships, acquire certain possessions, and make constructed choices of religious affiliation.

All of this is driven by the unconscious or semi-conscious need to build a man-made, soulishly influenced personality. Obviously then, it's the soul that needs more healing.

Remember, in this book we're talking about issues of the soul, *not* the spirit.

We're also *not* talking about the emotion of healthy shame. Some shame is good and God-given, which we have already discussed.

HOW DOES POISON FEEL?

From here on, the shame we'll be discussing is **unhealthy** and **toxic**. Before we explore some of the characteristics of toxic shame, I want you to understand from an educational point of view what those words mean. Webster's New World Dictionary defines "unhealthy" as sickly; not well; harmful to health; harmful to morals. Webster defines "toxic" as poisonous. We can see right away that unhealthy, toxic shame causes our emotions to be sickly; can damage our health; and can be poisonous to our morals. Experts believe that an excess of this emotion is poisonous to the whole being of a person, and that healing it leads to health in other emotions.

Shame is a very persuasive feeling that one is unworthy, inadequate, flawed, defective. In other words, one will never add up and is born to be a failure. When shame becomes chronic, good people that love God will carry around an inner inadequacy, a bad, questioning feeling about their self-validity. Even though they know they have peace with God, they consciously or unconsciously fight with this weakness, this subtle, low-grade feeling that can permeate thoughts and actions. It produces a low self-esteem. Shame is a deep sense of embarrassment, producing a feeling of wanting to hide, pull away, or not exist.

At the beginning of this chapter, I asked you to think about the most embarrassing moment of your life. I want you to take a moment and think about what I'm going to ask you now. What kind of feelings did it conjure up inside of you?

With the awareness of that feeling fresh in our thoughts, let's continue to talk about toxic shame. Unhealthy shame can occur when the emotion of shame gets built up to high levels inside a person because it is never processed or dealt with in a direct and proper way. It's when that feeling gets fixed somewhere and held on overload that it can become unhealthy or toxic. It produces a myriad of other feelings and can influence everything we do.

As I've said, "hide" is the key word when it comes to understanding shame. When I fell down those steps at the university, the feeling I had was to hide. That was a momentary common shame, and I got over it. But there are experiences that we have **where shame marks us on the inside.** Later in life, whatever triggers that feeling, or whatever circumstance surrounds that feeling inside of us, or whenever that shame manifests, it creates a painful empty feeling that makes us want to hide, even if we don't outwardly act on it.

Because shame is an emotion that tells us something about our identity, and if we feel it in toxic amounts somewhere in our soul that we're not too good, then we'll put up a mask and be something different than we really are. Why? Because we think if people see the way we really are, or the way we "feel" inside, they won't like us. So we revert to a mask that we've created. We'll talk about this in the following chapters.

That type of hiding paralyzes your confidence. Shame withers the spirit of a person. Shame destroys your will and poisons your relationships. It has become toxic to you. When that shame is in excess, it will mark every single part of your life, including your Christianity and your relationship with God. It affects your relationship with others and with the church. It hinders intimacy, because if you have a feeling of love or compassion toward someone, shame joins with it and causes you to be a little timid, or bound up, unable to express that compassion. You end up feeling bad about having a good emotion, and worse yet, can't express the good feeling.

IDENTITIES CREATED BY SHAME

Different people have different levels of shame in their lives. We all experience feelings in different ways. Something in a circumstance that might seem like a small thing to you, can really be painful to another. We're made up differently. So we can't judge the shame that another feels based on what we've been through. We've all been through hard things in life. Some have tasted of shame; others have their lives crippled by it, making them want to constantly avoid feeling the awful, empty feelings that touching that shame produces. Some are aware of what they are feeling; others aren't even aware they are feeling shame, yet it slowly seeps through the covers like a lethal gas. Clearly, hiding it doesn't alleviate it. Healing it does.

When you're experiencing toxic shame, you wish people weren't looking because you feel as though they can see through you. Sometimes the feeling can be so strong that you can literally think they will see you as you FEEL about yourself – even though others can't know how you're feeling. Of course, we all try to avoid it because it's an empty, dark, hollow, sometimes painful feeling; so we become experts at covering it up and hiding it so it doesn't manifest within us.

Remember that when emotions are healthy, they are to pass through you and teach you something when you are in touch with them. But when shame is somewhere in your being, an emotion or experience is unable to pass through. It has taken a central place in a part of your identity and instead, you will take experiences and internalize them. Shame will take an ordinary experience, twist it, and cause it to hit your self-worth; it attacks who you are as a person. The other emotions then get stuffed and go somewhere else.

Then shame can attach itself to every emotion that one has, so it becomes a core factor inside of someone's life. Total identities can be shame-based. Or, a specific area of your life may be filled with toxic shame. Some people act weak and timid; and others act very aggressive, very controlling, and very together. However the person acts, it's all to cover the shame. That's one of the main reasons why it's important to get shame in the right perspective, because **shame is one of the only emotions that deals with the core of your identity.** Guilt says our *behavior* is bad; shame says *we* are bad.

Let me give you some examples of the characteristics of identity-based shame. If you see yourself or any aspect of your life in any of these areas, then it could be that there is some unhealthy shame somewhere. Your personality is being warped and limited; and your true, God-given identity and inner peace is being muffled.

1. Feeling like an outsider
2. Being disconnected or lonely
3. Defensive
4. Perfectionist
5. Fear of intimacy and commitments
6. Sabotages or hurt friendships
7. Looking to always rescue others; getting stuck in dependent or co-dependent relationships
8. Shyness; feelings of inferiority or worthlessness
9. Social withdrawal
10. Anger
11. Jealousy
12. Judgmental attitudes; legalistic thinking
13. Difficulty in accepting forgiveness; in accepting gifts or receiving
14. Constantly feeling distant from God
15. Compulsive behavior to block painful feelings; addictions
16. Excuses, rationalizations, lies
17. Blames
18. Selfish; self-centered

The list can go on, even to suicidal tendencies. As you can see, shame sometimes moves beyond a feeling. It can have a set of physical responses like looking down, withdrawing, reacting, and unpredictable actions. It bears uncomfortable thoughts like, "I'm a failure in life," to the point of spiritual despair. It's very painful to believe in one's basic defection as a human being.

"I'M A BAD PERSON"

Toxic shame is like a silent, internal bleeding; it is inner torment. It carries a great sense of hopelessness. No matter what we do, *we* cannot correct it. Different from the emotion of guilt where we *can* fix a wrong, shame leaves us feeling helpless. Why? Because shame deals with your *being,* not your *doing.* Guilt has to do with your actions; but shame makes you feel that you *are* the problem. You can try to do something to get rid of shame, but you're *doing* doesn't get rid of it. There are people running around doing all kinds of things, unintentionally trying to ease the pain of shame. **But when it comes to toxic shame, it's only the power of the love of God that can set us free.** That's why the healing of inner shame is such a powerful experience, because to let God into your life, *you must let go.* The most powerful way to be healed from shame is surrender; and we'll discuss it later in this book.

Toxic shame forces us to feel isolated, lonely, as though we are the only ones that have this feeling. Unhealthy shame says, "I'm afraid to tell you about my shame because if I do, you'll think I'm bad. I can't stand hearing how bad I am, so I'll keep it to myself, block it, and pretend it's not there." Shame will make you critical. Shame makes you feel attacked when no one is trying to attack you.

You can recognize shame's voice because it bases its influence on these three concepts:

- **It's your fault**
- **You deserved it**
- **There is something wrong with you**

If you listen closely to the way you speak to yourself, to the thoughts that come to your mind, or the tone of the feelings you have in your soul, usually you can locate the road that leads to shame. Look for the "smell and taste" of the three concepts.

CAN LOVE HURT?

The most common way toxic shame enters is from any wound intentionally or unintentionally inflicted by someone we love, usually a primary caregiver in our lives. Shame goes from common to toxic in cases of physical, emotional, sexual, and spiritual abuse. It can become toxic from forms of neglect as well as different traumatic circumstances in life. Of course the level of toxicity varies from person to person, based on the extent or degree of how they were treated, their reactions, and the circumstances. Whatever the level, toxic shame is deadly and must be healed. We will look deeper into the family life later.

But I've got news for you. We can heal the shame! We can be delivered! We can be set free from it in the name of Jesus. We can walk in the healthy, natural emotion of shame, and get the excess removed from the inside of us.

Let me close this chapter by sharing some testimonies about how toxic shame works, and how emotional healing, through the light of the Lord, made these individuals whole.

THOUGHTS DISTORTED BY SHAME

Once as I was teaching in a church about shame, a man came to me and told me this story. He said that he had been a believer for many years, loved God with all his heart, and felt the call into the ministry. But, he had always fought with the plaguing and disturbing thought that he was a homosexual.

The man was very happily married with a very healthy intimate life, and he had wonderful kids. Even though he had never acted on the thought, somewhere inside was a deep fear about his sexuality.

He did all he could do to "take the thought captive," and even went through deliverance. All of this helped, but the breakthrough came when he understood what shame was and how it worked.

As he did some prayerful emotional work, he realized that his mind had created a thought to pacify a traumatic and shameful event from his past. He spoke openly about the event, named the shame, felt the feeling of the attached shame and all the other emotions included in the incident, and allowed them to follow their course through his soul by sharing them and expressing them with a safe and supportive person. As soon as the shame was healed, all the thoughts about his sexuality were settled. Today, he no longer fights with or is tempted by those shaming and abnormal thoughts about his sexuality. Toxic shame is a powerful emotion.

SHAME DISGUISED AS "GOD"

A friend shared with me about her soul being vexed and her thoughts twisted by what she later realized was shame. Her incident involved the ministry. She and her ex-husband had once pioneered a successful work; but he fell into sin, pushed her out of the church that she pioneered beside him, they divorced, and eventually the church closed.

For twelve years afterwards, she cried and remorsed whenever this region of the country was mentioned, thinking that God has given her a prayer burden for the region and the people. She felt some type of "void" inside of her that she thought would never be fulfilled. **She assumed that "void" was the call of God that she had failed in, and because of that, would always be resident within her.** During those years, her personality changed into one that was always driven to please others, fearing that she was not quite good enough and that someone might be disappointed in her for any given reason.

She spoke with several well-established ministers, but none knew how to effectively help her pertaining to the "void" inside. She received prayer after prayer, but continued to stuff the pain inside, vowing to be a warrior for God in spite of the odds. Repeatedly she attempted to "will" or confess all the bad feelings of hurt away. She did all she knew to do to become whole. God blessed her with a wonderful new husband, and not long after, another child; but the pain or the "void" never left until she realized the shroud of *lies* and exposed the shame that had kept her locked into this false concept.

Remember one of the statements shame speaks? It whispers, "Something is wrong with you." My friend had unintentionally believed it.

The void she described was shame. Once she *deeply* realized that she hadn't failed God, but instead had fulfilled her call with spiritual success, **she saw the shame, called it by name, and the "void" closed up inside of her.** The enemy could no longer take advantage; she was no longer shamed by believing she was a failure or that she had failed God. The painful, hopeless tears she thought was a prayer burden, but were really from the confused shame-ridden emotions she had inside, stopped. She no longer was driven to please everyone around her by trying to cover-up a "bad person" failure mentality.

A VOW OF SILENCE

Another Christian woman shared once that she had been sexually harassed (groping and intimidation) by a well-known minister that she respected and trusted. She was single at the time it happened, and had always had purity in her intimate relationships.

Right after the incident took place, she went to the bathroom to get herself together. She was so shaken, confused, and upset by this surprising and dark encounter, that she made a vow in that bathroom to deny the event, never to think about it, and to never tell anyone what had happened. She had to avoid the shamingly painful thoughts that this unsolicited occurrence was her fault, or that somehow she must have desired this type of undignified, ungodly treatment. Enter toxic shame.

After ten years of blocking out the past, the toxic emotions that had accumulated were surfacing. During a very significant dating relationship, the woman was plagued with thoughts and feelings that hindered her from a healthy connection with a man she thought she might marry.

Later, after getting the help she needed and releasing the pain and the toxic shame behind her secret, she realized something powerful. The emotional closeness and love in the relationship with the man she might marry had an "iron sharpen iron" effect on her emotions; it drew up her unresolved issues. Because the incident was so shaming to her, to share and release the emotions made her almost feel like she would rather die than tell. Once it was all out, she was free. They were able to heal her shame and the pain of the incident together, and today, she is well.

It's really interesting how quietly, but thoroughly toxic shame can influence our lives. **Whatever it takes, we need to address the shame issue and allow God to work deeply in our lives, our churches, our ministries, and the nations.**

Chapter 9

EVERY DAY SHAME IN OUR EMOTIONAL ENVIRONMENT

As I familiarize you with what shame is, my goal is to mention things that will help you identify more clearly the concepts and feelings that *make* shame what it is. In this chapter, I focus on what I will call common or every day shame. As you read, you will probably get a more accurate picture of what I am talking about. Later we will explore the primary source of shame – acquired shame that comes from family relationships. It's usually toxic from the family life, especially if it has come from any kind of neglect or abuse. But first, shame in our world.

SHAME AND THE CULTURE

Our culture carries a lot of shame. People will shame you because of your race. People will shame you because of your beliefs. Our culture teaches shame by violating the personal boundaries and preferences of others when it wasn't deserved. There's even an expression in our society where we say, "Shame on you."

Think of the competition in our culture. Competition can be very good. It can be motivational and teach values. But much of the competition in our culture carries shame with it. People are driven to get to the top. And if you don't make it to the top, you can be filled with shame and failure. To tell the truth, many of the people striving to get to the top may have a lid on some toxic shame that's really inside of them, driving them on to achieve and BE something. They are pushed to have to prove something, to be worth something. It all goes back to finding an identity.

Common shame can be apparent in our culture through peer pressure. How? Choosing who is popular and who isn't. That statement alone carries all sorts of examples with it. Teens feel they have to conform in image and appearance. If you don't have the right clothes in high school, then you are a nerd, a shame. Go to any high school today in America and look for the guy sitting off in the corner, plunking on his computer, eating a grilled cheese sandwich, with a duddy little hair cut. He feels bad about who he is as a good guy who likes computers – nothing wrong with that. It's okay, it's positive; but shame may blind him to who he really is and what he can do with his life. He's probably battling some defeating thoughts while the others snicker and say, "Computer nerd, computer nerd."

There's a lot of prejudice in our culture and that produces shame. Some people are ashamed of being black. Some people are ashamed of being white; or Hispanic; a Native American Indian, or oriental. It's the nature of their birth! They have no control over it. God made them that way; yet if they allow it, they are ashamed because of the stigmatism that's in our culture.

Unhealthy shame is in our culture. And sometimes when it's in the culture, it can unconsciously get in us. It can also occur from some of the relationships and events that have happened in your life. How many times have we seen that, even as Christians, people are shamed when they go through a divorce? Some people carry that shame for the rest of their lives; not only because of the emotional pain involved, but because others mark them "divorced" as though they have a plague.

My stand on divorce is this. God hates it, and the reason He hates it is not because the couple is not married. God hates it because the events leading to the divorce and the divorce process itself can devastate the emotional lives of the couple and their children. God hates it when people *hurt* in any way. Divorce can be one of the most painful emotional experiences any human being can ever experience, and some people never fully recover from its effect. If it happens, God will forgive it and heal it. We should never cast anyone out because they've been divorced. If Jesus can forgive murder, then He can certainly forgive divorce. It's only the men, the women, and a religious system which thrives on shame that will put that kind of unhealthy mark on others for a painful mistake that happened in their lives.

DON'T ACCEPT IT

Shame is accepting fault or responsibility for something that is not yours. Did you catch that? **Shame is accepting responsibility or internalizing, receiving pain, rejection, whatever it is, for something that you have no control over, or just plain didn't do it.**

The devil will try to tell you that you deserved it. That's how shame works. You'll unconsciously accept thoughts like, "Well, I guess I deserve it."

None of us deserve it! Jesus took it, despised it, and conquered it so we don't have to take it. But the enemy tells you that you deserved it because you're too short or too tall; because you're ugly, or too skinny, or too fat. You think that you have this certain bent in life, or you're a certain color and on and on. If you accept the shame, it can build up in you as it is internalized through life, and it can cause you to become insecure in everything you do.

People will shame you because of certain choices you make. Sometimes shame is used to manipulate others. For example, let's say that you go to an amusement park and everyone wants to ride the double roll-over roller coaster – everyone but you. If you don't go on that ride, the others will walk a few feet ahead of you and cut you off emotionally because you didn't take part in their party. They will judge you and make you feel dumb or weird. You have the right to go on that ride or stay off it and still be loved. It's your choice and there should be no shame induced on individuals for their individual personal preferences.

CAN YOU BELIEVE IT . . . SHAME IN THE CHURCH?

Some people even use shame to get someone to go to church! "If you don't come to church, bless God..." So the people come because they didn't want to feel shamed. They didn't come because the Holy Spirit led them, or by their own choice. They came so everyone would see them there, or because they would get the third degree if they didn't show up. I wonder how many people attended church today because they had shamed themselves or were pressured by a pastor or by the leadership? Maybe some didn't show up because of their shame. They were afraid that people might see what they're trying to hide, how they are feeling about themselves, or their inadequacies. Some of the "no showers" have an attitude (when they do show up) of "Don't confront me, don't control me. I do what I want." It's crazy the different attitudes that we can develop over our good behavior and our unacceptable behavior!

To be fair, I understand that backslidden Christians must choose to heal themselves and grow up in Christ, no matter what others say or think. Some people will blame a pastor for something he did twenty years ago. They must get out of this blame mentality and learn to forgive. There also must come a place for respect of authority. At the same time, maybe the pastor didn't make a mistake. All of us must realize and recognize that some people just don't have it together. A leadership role or holding a position in a church doesn't guarantee the leader is emotionally healthy. Whether a leader in your life is healthy or not doesn't have to affect your relationship with God. Heal all of that stuff and move on!

Some ministers cannot be secure with the size of their church, or the impact of their ministry because they are shame-based. They think that something is wrong with them, or that others think something is wrong with them, if their church is small or they aren't building a new building. What those ministers are saying is, "You must accept me because I have big numbers." You don't need big numbers to be accepted. Or, "You must accept me because I have an anointing."

I don't have to be accepted on whether I have an anointing in a certain area or not. But if I have toxic shame *inside*, then I have a low self-esteem and do things to avoid my bad feelings or letting you see the real me. Consciously or unconsciously I start to think something is wrong with me. It's a terrible feeling. I have to cover those insecurities with a false mask to look good. My soul needs to construct a personality that is "ministry approved." But if my insecurities are discovered and touched, it can connect with those issues inside of me and there can be emotional trouble, either for me or the people around me.

SHAME AND THE FEELINGS OF DISGRACE

There are a variety of circumstances in life that carry the shame stigma. Experiencing a death can sometimes carry shame. Was it my fault? Did I deserve to lose that person? Different sicknesses can produce shame. A bankruptcy, something that happens at your job, or work relationships. You don't want to internalize these lies and feelings so that they become something more.

If you're single and sitting at home, wondering what's wrong with you because everyone else is out on a date and having fun, that's self-shame. Many times our self-shaming thoughts and behavior become automatic thinking. Those thoughts destroy us and eventually, our relationships. They cause us to withdraw from people and from God. When excess, emotional shame is healed on the inside of you, it rids you of the hidden shame that's laced your thoughts. Your mind can be clear and free!

Current relationships where there's bickering, fighting, and putting each other down all the time releases shame. Usually shamed people shame each other, and everyone living in their house is shamed and afraid as well. There can be rage, anger, bitterness, and withdrawal. Sometimes there is abuse. And of course, the shame from any kind of abuse becomes toxic.

It's no fun growing up in a house where there is verbal abuse going on, and where inflicting pain has become a way of life. Some families have such a shame structure that they really can't help being vindictive and hurtful to the others around them. There are Christians who portray this type of behavior at home, then cart their families off to praise the Lord on Sundays. We need to be healed.

SHAME DIGS A LARGE HOLE

Maybe there were specific events that were very traumatic and damaging to you where you internalized the feelings of the experience, and the internal feelings created a place, a hole in you, an empty place filled with toxic emotions and shame. When you became born-again, Jesus filled many of those places for you. But there still may be some more that needs healing. We all have some light scars that cover unhealed wounds. Not every event, person, or situation causes shame, but we all have sensitive issues in our souls that deserve some investigation and attention.

To the degree that we internalize the emotions of our experiences, they can attach to the core of who you are. If the toxic shame level is reached, it can become an identity. That's important for you to understand.

Many specialists believe that toxic shame is the number one cultural sickness in America. Almost every addictive problem comes from shame. We'll discuss those in more detail later. Almost every co-dependent family problem usually gets down to some shame issues.

Let's explore a source where shame can begin and become very toxic. Let's go back to our family roots.

Chapter 10

ORIGINAL FAMILY LIFE

Our families are interesting, aren't they? It is clear that all of us inherit certain physical traits from our family line. Most of our emotional foundation, emotional make-up, and behavior traits comes from our family roots as well.

The Bible is clear about how spiritual qualities and tendencies are transmitted to us from our parents or our ancestral line. We've discussed that Timothy's strong faith was imparted to him by being around his grandmother and mother; but also because there was a spiritual endowment that his family line carried.

Generational curses are also carried through family lines as well, and need to be broken through prayer, ministry, and a godly lifestyle. Some believers are spiritually ignorant, held in what seems like invisible, yet tangible bondages that dissipate when handled in the power of God. I strongly endorse any ministry in your life that breaks spiritual powers over you and helps to release you from generational habits and traits that are destructive.

In many instances, emotional healing comes with addressing an issue spiritually. Yet some emotional habits have no spiritual root at all. And, sometimes after the spiritual part is dealt with, the soul then needs to be healed and restored from the effects of the spiritual influence. Whatever the case, it is very important for you to understand your emotions, and be sure that your emotional life is completely healed.

If you look closely enough at your family's emotional life and habits, you may see where you may have inherited some very good qualities, but also some toxic emotions. Usually toxic shame originates interpersonally, primarily in significant relationships. These relationships are our source relationships, which occur in our present, original family.

Our parents have also handed down to us and helped to create an emotional root system in our lives as well. These emotional roots are the part of our soul that is very deep – the embedded part, or the very source of our emotional being. Sometimes those roots are unhealthy simply because of what we *learned* or didn't learn at home; what we *perceived* or didn't perceive; or what we *acquired* or didn't acquire from our parents.

Let me point out that I am well aware the Bible says in 2 Corinthians 5:17, that we are "new creations" in Christ. I believe it in it's proper application and as a foundation to pursue victory. Yet there are many emotional scars that are not miraculously removed through a salvation experience. However dedicated Christian people may seem, some have major interpersonal problems. Like one author said, *"New creatures, old pain."*

DON'T PLAY THE BLAME GAME

Before we explore this subject further, I want to make something very clear. No matter what you are going through today, we as a society, in most cases, have no right to go back and blame our parents. Playing the role of a victim is an easy way out. It can be hard to see and acknowledge our own parent's weaknesses, because every child wants his/her parents to be perfect. Although a lot of parents are operating out of their own inherited shame, emotional scars, dysfunction, failures, and weakness, they're doing the best they can. Through forgiveness and God's light, respect them and understand that they have weaknesses as all do. Nevertheless, you must be mature and accept the responsibility to heal your shame apart from what they did or didn't do during your childhood. Your destiny is in your own hands now.

The enemy has a calculated plan for people's lives. I've decided that I'm not going to let any spiritual entity wreck my life through *anything* that is put on my life, no matter where it came from.

I know the successes or failures in my life are not based on my childhood. I love my parents with a passion and will always be appropriately loyal to them. My life is not dictated by what they did or didn't do. They raised me the best they knew how, gave me what they had to give, and they did a good job.

I refuse to be shipwrecked by thinking, "Well, my problem is because my dad did this and my dad did that." My father loves me, and he did the very, very best he could in raising me. The issues are not with our parents. The issue has to do with the whole concept of shame and how it works. Most shame is transferred from generation to generation. The bottom line is this: **If you didn't have the parents you had, you would have had another set who would have exposed you to a different type of shame.**

This chapter could really be a book in itself. Although there is much detailed information that I cannot discuss here, I do want to bring out a very simple and basic understanding of how important the family of origin is to our emotional make-up as adults. It deserves some attention and study.

CHILDREN ARE VULNERABLE

The emotional life of a child is shaped by what we do and by what we project as the primary care-giving parent. A child has no defenses. They're not supposed to. They are innocent and vulnerable. They internalize and absorb the attitudes, actions, and unspoken expectations of their parents. They will automatically receive what you project to them because they have no filters. They were created by God to pattern their lives by what they see in their parents.

A precious little child is created to be extremely vulnerable, just like Adam and Eve were vulnerable to God in the garden. First of all, children were created to trust. The second thing is that they were created to feel the environment around them, to be open, and from that environment, to develop emotional responses and habits.

You can see that a normal, healthy child is like a little sponge. That child will absorb everything that the family puts into her/him. They will record every action. Just as the child can experience love and joy within a family, he/she can also feel family pain. If there is any significant or unrelieved pain and tension within a family, the child can feel that pain. Children also develop according to how they are treated.

Sometimes children are helpless victims of verbal, physical, or sexual abuse which tragically, can emotionally damage children for life unless it is healed. As I've stated, every kind of abuse leaves toxic emotions with it. No matter how much we want to protect our children, they are very, very sensitive. If it's not explained or handled properly by the caregivers in the child's life, then some of that pain and tension can be internalized within the child. When the environment lacks the proper nurturing essential to healing emotional development, children experience injury and abandonment. Of course, no one can say when the shame from an incident actually becomes toxic, but it is always something to think and pray about.

Some of the things we bear as adults today are from wounds in our childhood. Unhealthy shame comes from what we do with the negative messages, negative affirmations, beliefs, and rules that we hear growing up. People who have suffered physically, sexually, and emotionally – sometimes because of the reality of their scars – have difficulty overcoming such deep wounds.

A child is usually healthy enough to feel much like Adam and Eve did before the fall. If at times chaos is around them, it usually passes through them because they are open and free and are not ashamed. But if the situation stays chaotic enough, or becomes traumatic, they will automatically start to feel that the problems in the home are somehow their fault or responsibility.

If mom and dad had unsettled toxic shame within them, eventually they are going to release it in the home in some fashion. If mom is on another one of her rampages, she may say to her small son in an abusive way, "You're always getting into trouble. There's something wrong with you. You'll never amount to anything." **Those words need to be broken over your life, but the feelings and the scars that can come with them needs to be healed as well.**

Think for a moment what those words do to a child who doesn't yet have his defenses developed – he's not supposed to be developed yet. The first stage of life is to trust his primary caregiver. If her words are always critical and demeaning, the small boy will internalize those statements. He trusts his caregiver; so he believes what she says is true about him.

YOU ARE A MIRROR

Parents are mirrors to their children. In other words, the children will become what they see in the parent. Children unknowingly internalize feeling emotionally abandoned and neglected when the parent cannot mirror or affirm their child's emotional needs, because of toxic shame or their own overwhelming emotional needs.

We need "mirrors" in our lives. Sometime today, you probably used a mirror to see yourself because it was very helpful to you. The Bible calls the Word of God a mirror, a reflection of your life. The mirror helps to reflect an image that we see. The mirror defines for us our identity.

For most of us, we need to replace the mirrors in walls of our minds because the picture we see of ourselves has been distorted. Many times the distortion came from family situations, and is the result of what we were given as children.

Do you remember when you went to the State Fair, and you found those mirrors that had bumps in them? If you stood before one of them, you were so skinny because your legs were as tall as the ceiling! The top of your body was as wide as a roof, and you'd stand and make faces in it!

Then you'd go to the next mirror, and it looked like you were under three feet tall with legs that looked like little tree trunks!

Those mirrors were a distorted reality of what you really were. The different situations we experience in childhood create mirrors in our minds. But some of those mirrors were like the ones at the State Fair – they create distortion and illusion. The problem comes when you look into that distorted mirror and think it's normal. Those mirrors have a dramatic influence on many parts of our adult lives, including our decisions and behaviors. They form the kind of work we will do, our relationships, our response to stress, who we'll marry, our education. Why? Because we make those kinds of decisions based on who we are, and if we have a distorted image, a misplaced identity of who we really are, then we can continually make the wrong decisions and live dysfunctionally as an adult.

Why do we need mirrors? Because we need reflections in our lives to help us get the right identity. We need self-awareness; we need to know who we are, what we're worth, what we need, and how to get it. A child needs that from the parent. But when a parent can't give that, or gives something else instead, then the mirrors turn out to reflect a little stubby guy, or a long distorted picture. Because parents are the mirrors that reflect who you are and what you're worth, if the emotional nurturing was lacking or negative, the shame and the scars from that experience were produced from your family of origin. God can heal every level of toxic shame, and all the scars, no matter how deep or no matter where they came from!

FAMILY SKELETONS

Think about the shame we produce in our children without even realizing it. For example, let's say a little girl noticed that her mom was crying on and off all day, lying in the bed, too sad to go to work. It has happened many times, but this time is the worst.

The little girl wants her father to call the doctor, but what does the Father answer? "No, honey. We live in a small town and what would people say if they knew your mom was sick?" The family rule of silence is really promoting and creating secrets and shame.

Or how about the Christian family who tried to look so together in the eyes of the church? One day, dad got mad and hit the wall with his fist. "Don't ever tell anyone that dad got that mad," mom warns. She didn't want anyone at the church to ever know or to think they were less than the perfect example of a Christian family. Now, you never show anger because you think it's shameful, and if you do show it, you can deeply shame yourself.

Teaching children to keep family secrets breeds shame. Secrets don't have to be extraordinary to be powerful. They only have to remain secret. They can be simple, but they are always significant. I'm not saying to throw discretion to the wind, but secrets produce a stigma of shame. The shame then develops a life of secrecy, hypocrisy, and judgmentalism in our children.

When families are carrying shame, wounds, and other toxic emotions, it's not a safe place to be real. If you can't be your true self in a wounded family, then it's going to be hard to express emotion in a healthy way. **Do you realize that your emotional life will affect the life of your children or your future children?**

UNSPOKEN RULES SPEAK LOUDLY

My emotional life has been affected by the emotional life of my parents and my grandparents. My emotional life will affect my children, my nieces and nephews – all those that I have the chance to be a primary caregiver to. It will also affect my marriage.

The worst thing parents can do is to ignore their emotional or spiritual lives. The emotional realm is very powerful and very important in establishing the family. So what I do or don't do in the emotional realm affects people around me. It's very important that we become well and whole in the emotional area.

Remember, shame is an emotion that tells you about who you are as a person; and much of that shame we unintentionally accepted while we were children. I'm sure you can see that in an abusive, wounded, or dysfunctional family, shame abounds. There are different unspoken RULES that each family sets up in order to deal with that shame, that actually work to keep the shame hidden but alive. The more rigid and enforced the rule, the more possibility for toxic, emotional fall-out.

#1: BE BLIND AND BE QUIET
(**Don't see, acknowledge, or discover anything; and certainly don't TALK!**)

No family actually sits down to have a family committee meeting and says, "All right. Let's all be blind." No, usually that rule is unspoken. It just kind of hangs in the atmosphere, and for generations people have lived by it. According to this rule, the family will expect you to be blind to your own perceptions of reality. There's no need to point out problems, situations, or mistakes so that correction can be made. This rule says to just act like you don't see problems or situations and to just continue on.

This unspoken rule prohibits the full expression of feelings, desires, and needs.

Can the blindness hinder you from seeing what is not healthy in your life or your background? Usually it takes God or someone else, like a close friend, a spouse, a mentor, a good book by a sound person, the Bible, or someone else to show you what is healthy. It's not normal or healthy to be blind to your own perceptions of reality, or to be quiet about it. *The reality of the presence of these rules will usually surface in the most intimate and significant relationships in our lives. People we allow to be close to us, will see close.*

Most of us have heard the statement, "Be quiet. Don't discuss family problems with anyone." Why? For many families, individuals, and churches, the most important concern is reputation. If we discuss problems, it brings shame; and no one likes shame. No one likes to feel bad about themselves or think that someone else feels bad about them either. What would the neighbors think? What will my mother think if you bring that into my house? What will the boss think? What will the pastor think? What will other preachers think? What will the other members do? It's sad, because the enemy uses these lies to tie a noose around our necks so we won't face reality.

"Well, there never was a problem with alcoholism in our family. No way. Grandpa just had a problem with walking straight. He had a problem with his leg."

To this family it would be shameful to admit that grandpa was an alcoholic. They don't want to bring the shame and the family pain into the light so it can be healed.

Any number of issues may be hidden. A relative's senility, mother's pill dependency, father's problems at work, trouble with a son or daughter, or trouble with the law, abortion, disease, incest, any kind of abuse, homicide, suicide, financial disaster, and so on. Children in these types of families are told either directly or indirectly they shouldn't talk about any of these things. If they do, they will be punished for bringing shame to the family. Therefore, no one speaks of his/her desires, needs, wants, or feelings.

Children who have been groomed with this unspoken rule can be either full of anger or have a doormat personality. They can have a low-grade depression because they lost who they really are; or a people-pleaser, looking for acceptance. They also have a tendency to be withdrawn from public life, or passive about situations in life. Why? Because they were unable to express themselves. To them, expression itself may create feelings of shame.

You'll also find that people who were raised in this type of atmosphere have a hard time communicating. They were never allowed to express how they felt without incurring heaps of shame for it! It was easier to be quiet than to take the shame.

Let's heal the shame so you can express what you want and what you need. That's healthy.

#2: BE NUMB

Some families don't want you to feel anything, and they certainly don't like it if you have personal boundaries they aren't allowed to cross over into. If mom and dad didn't have personal boundaries because their mom and dad didn't have them, then trouble comes if someone else in the family establishes them.

Boundaries are important because they protect us. If certain boundaries are crossed, and someone comes into a space that is privately yours, that can be a violation. It can be wounding to you as a person.

We have to learn what boundaries are. Sometimes it's easier for a family to just be numb and not establish any boundaries at all. They step all over each other and don't even realize it. What's worse, they feel it's okay to do so. It would be an obvious survival tactic to be numb if everyone was walking all over you.

#3: DON'T TRUST ANYONE

This rule is interesting and has many facets to it that we won't discuss here; but a shame-filled family can say through actions and words, "Don't trust anyone. You should be suspicious of everyone." They tell you that everyone will hurt you, let you down, or is out to get something from you. Don't let anyone in. Don't let anyone know you or really see you. Sometimes this rule says that the *only* people you can trust is your immediate family, which creates tremendous obligation and isolation.

It's not my intention to be heartless, but what will happen to you when your immediate family physically dies, or whenever they abandon you? Then what will you do? Who will you trust?

This emotion-binding rule says not to trust anyone and that way, you'll never be disappointed. If you allow it, this distrust cycle can go on and on through many generations. It can even influence your relationship with God. That concept is totally dysfunctional and sets you up for a life of mistrust and insecurity.

#4: BE GOOD / BE PERFECT

This unspoken rule says to be good or be perfect because it pays. The result is that you are on guard of every action, of every behavior. It sets you up to always try to reach a level you will never reach. It puts a fear of failure inside of you, because if you don't always win, then you weren't good or perfect enough.

This unspoken rule also says that one must always be right in everything he/she does. Can you see how this lofty rule sets you up for disappointment and a poor, internal self-image? No one is able to be right all the time. We're human beings! Yet in this dysfunctional, unspoken rule, the family members attempt to live according to an externalized image, thus creating a performance mentality.

Can you imagine what it does to relationships? It is very hard to live under the critical eye of a perfectionist, and difficult to communicate with someone who has the need to always be right. Many super-achievers are covering a base of shame in their lives.

This unspoken rule also denies you five basic freedoms as a human being: the freedom to perceive, think, feel, desire, and imagine. In other words, in this type of house, you shouldn't think the way you do; you shouldn't have your personal feelings or desires, or use your imagination the way you do. Everything should be done the way the perfectionalistic person demands.

#5: BE IN CONTROL

This unspoken rule says that everyone in the family must be in control of all situations, interactions, feelings, and personal behavior. In their unspoken behavior, this family wants you to always have it together – after all, whatever you go through doesn't really hurt. To them, it's of utmost importance that one never betrays the family stigma, or the controlling person who considers themselves the central figure of the family life.

If you can't always be in control, then this rule has a double standard. It says to cover-up your own mistakes and if someone else makes an error, shame him – because shaming him makes you look better. Control combined with blame are major defense strategies a controller uses to cover their own shame. After being around a controlling person, it's easy to become a controller yourself.

Why is blame so important in a control-based family? Because blame maintains the balance to their dysfunctional system when their control is broken.

IT'S NEVER TOO LATE TO CHANGE

All of these mentalities create an environment that could be emotionally damaging to any normal child.

You may have your own list of unspoken rules. The good news is that it's never too late to recognize them and heal yourself from the emotional distortions and pain that they have created in your life. God will always make up for what you didn't get at home. You may even get to the point where you can sit around the table and laugh about the dark and hidden rules that have now come to light, and how glorious it *feels* not to experience the fruit of them in your life!

Before you can get to that step, we must all own up to the fact that most of us grew up in somewhat dysfunctional families. Of course, many people turn out very well adjusted anyway; but some sort of dysfunctional behavior is usually present in most homes. The important thing to realize is that because of those unspoken rules, some of us are carrying unhealed hurts, injured emotions, and toxic shame in our adult lives.

One of the best books I've read on the subject is called <u>Secrets of Your Family Tree: Healing For Adult Children of Dysfunctional Families</u>, (see Suggested Reading). It is written from a biblical perspective and I highly recommend it for those who want to grasp a deeper understanding on this vital subject of family dysfunction.

Let's discuss how these unspoken, dysfunctional rules came into being and why they have laced our lives.

Chapter 11

LOVE TANKS

It can be fun to laugh about the unspoken rules in our families; but at the same time, it's really important to closely inspect the rules to see how our family life has molded us. It's difficult but vital to see where we might have been hurt and negatively influenced by the lifestyle of our families. Some shameful situations aren't a laughing matter. Some shameful situations are very painful, and they need the grace of God to heal. There is an ample amount of grace available; but first, we have to be honest with ourselves, to allow God to show us what was really there, to accept and to heal the unhealthy emotional habits and influences of our childhood.

Hurts that aren't *acknowledged* can't be healed. Shame must be NAMED to be healed.

That statement is very important. Your healing begins with your acknowledging where you've been influenced and affected, and the consequences that some of those thoughts and some of those actions have had on you and produced inside you.

Remember, shame becomes toxic and affects the other emotions when it moves from common shame to something dark and dangerous on the inside. The place where we were mistreated, mishandled, discounted, or disgraced as a person becomes a mark within. Then deep inside, as the wound talks to us that we are not worthy, as adults we begin to mistreat and devalue ourselves. We then carry our own toxic shame and continue to shame ourselves. We can unintentionally read it into everything and allow it to make a personal statement about ourselves or to ourselves. It is time to heal it.

The problem is that we unknowingly spend most of our lives covering over the hurts and experiences of our pasts. There are different ways to make progress with healing, and some have begun the process. Finding a relationship with God and developing a strong spiritual life is the first step. Wherever you are now in your healing process, although things take time, the Holy Spirit can always take you to another level. He will set you free, completely.

In this chapter, we need to see why and how those dysfunctional rules got started in our families to begin with. Again, I define **dysfunction** as simply patterns, habits, and behaviors that "don't function," thus leading to unhealthy relationships and distorted emotions. It leads to codependence, which is a state where we turn our responsibility for our life and happiness over to our ego and to other people.

In most cases, dysfunction is not a pre-meditated thing. If people don't get help and they don't get healed, then they end up coping the best they can. We are to a point where we can't cope much longer because even Christian marriages are struggling, and many good Christian people are revealing their personal inner struggles. I think there are a lot of Christian people who really love God, conquer sin and disobedience daily, wage good warfare on the devil, but continue to live on the unsatisfying edge of defeat, simply because of dysfunctional, learned behaviors, beliefs, and feelings. The most sobering outcome of unhealthy emotions caused by dysfunction, is that child after child may be affected, and when they become parents, the entire generation is lacking emotionally.

HEALTHY HONOR

Before we go any further, I want to make it clear that we don't disown or dishonor our families because we feel they've hurt us, or let us down by modeling dysfunctional behavior to us. You may have to go so far as to distance yourself from your family and all its "craziness," but we won't get into the blame game. Remember, one of the most powerful covers and denial tactics for shame is blame towards others for our own weaknesses or shortcomings.

When we recognize and then own up to our individual shame and hurts, then healing and freedom will come. When we blame others for our condition, then those hurts remain intact within us, thus influencing our lives. Blame becomes an excuse that allows some of the turbulence in our lives.

It takes courage and it takes maturity to face up to your own problems, no matter how or where they started. You are an adult, and you have the freedom and the choice to allow God to heal you and set your life in order. That choice will not only benefit you today, but will benefit the future generations in your family, especially your own children. That's reason enough to do some significant soul-searching and healing. There may be more healing to do.

DOES IT AFFECT YOUR DESTINY WITH GOD?

God commanded us to *leave* our father and mother when we get married, but He never said to *disown* them. I believe leaving mother and father is also a command, not only in marriage, but when we walk with God to fulfill our destinies as well.

Here's a key: **Don't *disown* or abandon your mother and father because of dysfunctional behavior; instead *leave* the strongholds from the family of origin that cripple your personal wholeness and hold you back from fulfilling your destiny.**

What did Jesus say about fulfilling your destiny? We can read in Mark 10:29, 30 where He said we would need to leave our brothers, sisters, father, mother, wife, and children for the gospel's sake. But do you think He's really saying to disown them, forsake them, or leave them on their own before you can fulfill your destiny with Him? **No!**

Do you think He's saying that I have to hate my brother physically or with an emotion before I can fulfill the will of God for my life? **No!**

Allow me to use this simple illustration. I don't hate my brother; I love my brother. He's a part of my family! But any dysfunction, or any of the emotional bondage that may have entangled my life because of the close contact we had as siblings, **that's what I have to leave in order to go on with God.**

I have to be willing to allow the Holy Spirit to search my soul and my heart and bring illumination to me so that I know which strongholds of the family hold me down. What part of the dysfunctional family patterns influenced me? How has the codependence injured me? This procedure can be one of the ways we go on with God. No matter where you came from, how you were raised, or what kinds of unhealthy situations you have encountered, you *can* fulfill the destiny that God has given to you. You must *choose* to love and not blame; and to leave the emotional image of shame that has kept you bound, regardless of where it originated. That's not easy to do without God's help. And many times you need others in your life to help you as well.

IT'S THE NATURE OF LIFE

As every home is individual in it's character, so each family has its varying forms and degrees of dysfunctional, unhealthy behavior that influences everyone in that home. **It happens unintentionally, because it's the natural by-product of chaotic family life.**

Most parents will do the very best they can. I understand that there are cases of intentional neglect, but I believe that in the heart of any parent there is a desire to do the best he/she could do for their children. No parent wants to intentionally deprive a child, but it happens. Remember, your own parents had their emotional needs filled by their parents. If a parent wasn't nurtured, he/she won't have a lot of nurturing ability to meet the child's needs; unless, of course, the lack of it in the parent's lives is understood, acknowledged, and they work to improve and heal it.

You can look back through your family tree as far as you wish to go; but if you want to see the reason of behavior in your own parent's lives, you can usually start with your grandparents.

Understand that I'm not promoting a "victim mentality." I think we're a little tired of hearing that someone's problems came from what mom and dad did or didn't do. Some people never deal with their pain because it's so easy, in their own pain, to project it upon someone else.

The truth is, problems come because we're human beings and that's the nature of life. We don't live in a spiritually perfected earth. We have an enemy. We live with fallen people. Problems *do* come while we live in the earth.

No one is exempt from them. While you must refuse to be a victim of your past, it's also true that your past *does* mark you. So our job is to understand it, allow God to heal it, and go on.

If you're a parent, you don't have to be under fear thinking that you'd better hurry up and get your life together to be adequate; however, it *is* important for you to become healthy. I strongly encourage you to explore and heal. I applaud you for your effort. Where you know there is lack in your life, God can and will make up for the difference.

HEALTHY TANKS

In your mind, picture a tank with inches or meters of measurement written on the side. Now imagine the tank to be filled at various levels. It may be filled to the brim, or might measure very low. This example of a tank I'll refer to as a love tank, illustrating degree of healthy emotions and satisfied needs within a person. When I speak of filling the love tanks, I'm talking about the ease and ability we have as individuals to express and receive healthy emotions with others. The degree of measurement, I call emotional capacity or ability to function with healthy emotions.

In God's normal, ideal family, mom and dad's love tank should be connected to each other. They are filling one another emotionally, nurturing each other's love tanks with consistent mutual love, friendship, and respect. As they ultimately receive nurturing from God, in return, those elements they give to each other keep them nourished and provide a healthy and safe, emotional atmosphere for their children. By receiving from God first, they are able to keep their emotional tanks full so they can meet each other's needs and then give to the child.

In fact, walking closely with God and with each other in a healthy relationship, their love tanks can stay relatively full. Mom and dad will still have a few weaknesses and insecurities. They will also experience needy times as they face life's challenges. Being a Christian doesn't make one perfect, of course. As parents get their emotional tanks filled by God, and as they strive to give a lot of love to their children, even when uncomfortable and emotionally-draining circumstances may arise to challenge family life, the children continue to know they are loved and valuable, and nurturing continues. They can remain secure in a healthy, stable environment.

With a full love tank, mom and dad aren't needy; so the children don't grow up to be needy. The children don't strive throughout their childhood to get their needs met, or withdraw and protect themselves emotionally to survive, because the love tanks of the parents are full. As mom and dad openly and honestly deal with the issues in their personal lives, they can relate to each other and keep the tanks full. They can also model healthy emotional and relational habits so the kids develop relatively, well-adjusted, and stable.

WHEN THE TANKS ARE LOW

Let's face it, everyone goes into a marriage with good intentions, but not always free from emotional baggage or the willingness to deal with conflict when it surfaces. So, let's say that there is some sort of unhappiness between mom and dad. Maybe dad is gone a lot, or dad is unavailable for whatever reason. In that family situation, the parent's emotional tanks might not be totally filled, so in their own pain and lack, they aren't able to nurture the child. That leaves the emotional love tank on a very low level for the child. If it is not corrected, he/she enters adult life with a low emotional level. When a child enters adulthood with a low emotional level, it simply means they had unmet needs that were supposed to have been met at home by mom and dad.

The abandonment they feel inside is covered many different ways in their adult world. If the pain was felt to the level that it became toxic, the adult child tries to cover the pain in several ways, including addictions. Or, an adult can become particularly "needy" in areas that only God can fill.

Maybe dad had his particular addictions or ways he protected himself from feeling his own shame. Because dad can't meet mom's needs anymore, mom gets an unhealthy bond to the child and tries to get her needs met there. Unconsciously, she develops a demand on the child's love tank to meet her needs and desires.

Is a child capable of doing that? No. So the child goes through life not knowing what it is like to emotionally receive from mom and dad. They are stretched emotionally because they were "taken from" as children when they needed to be given to. They are wounded. And because they are wounded, they are in pain.

A 15-YEAR-OLD ADULT

I remember working with someone, and the conversation came to where I once asked how she really felt inside. This was an adult. Her answer surprised me.

"You know how I really feel?" she began. "I feel like I'm 15, because when I was that age, my mom placed such a demand on me to meet her needs, I felt like it just drained everything out of me." This person wanted to go further to clearly identify her issues so that God could heal her and make up for the lack that she felt in her emotional and mental development.

She continued. "I still feel like I'm 15 inside. I really need God to help me and heal me because of what I missed." At fifteen years old, she felt responsible to meet her mother's needs and to fulfill the emotional lack in her parent's life. Now even in her adulthood, her mother continues to make a demand for a very strong place in her life. This is unhealthy.

Have you ever met adults that when you really get to know them, or when they get under pressure and into conflict, they act like immature teenagers? Or perhaps they seem so nice, but when they don't get what they want in their personal relationships, they lash out in anger, bitterness, abuse, or weakness? Maybe they withdraw, or press further into their addictive behavior. That's because that is what they *really* have going on inside of them. They have all kinds of mixed up emotions, many unmet needs, and areas that were never nurtured or developed in their lives. They can function as adults to a certain level, but not very well in some cases. Their reactions may not all be toxic, but the behavior probably deserves to be looked into for potential healing.

We all have areas we can grow, but I am convinced that some areas need some special attention and a time of serious focus to get a hold of, understand thoroughly, and heal the pain and the shame. It is possible to heal everything to the point that those weaknesses don't dominate life or destroy you and the people around you – including your children.

GOOD OR BAD, IT *WILL* TRANSFER

We touched on it earlier in the book, but if mom and dad carry unresolved issues, these things or the results of these issues can be transferred to the children, just by association. We know that it's true with spiritual things. Timothy had faith that was instilled or transferred into him by his association with his grandmother and mother. What is inside of your pastor can be transferred into you; not just spiritual things, but attitudes and ways of relating to people. That's one reason why a pastor must stay clean in spirit, be open to change, and very accountable. Whatever is in a leader's being will flow out to the people. As a parent, what's in your being can flow out to your children.

That's why it's so important to rid yourself of your acquired family shame and heal any inner wounds so its fruit is not passed on at any level or degree, like a hot potato from generation to generation.

Remember what we discussed in the family of origin chapter? A child can be severely restricted because of unmet needs. There can be a childish part of adults that are like hungry little monsters. As an adult, whenever their wounds surface, all those unmet needs are like little monsters that manifest in different ways. We must learn to heal, feed, and nurture those areas so that they're not monsters anymore, but friends. As friends, those feelings will be in the right place, in their right balance inside of us. Only God can do that for us.

Remember that any significant, unrelieved pain, tension, or difficulty within a family, the child will feel. No matter how much we want to protect our children, they are very, very sensitive and they internalize and interpret a lot. The children may not know what they are feeling or why, but it develops them emotionally. Many of the repetitive problems we experience as adults are connected to unresolved childhood issues.

DID YOU THINK THE FAULT WAS YOURS?

Problems within our family life can create emotional discomfort and need in a child. Let's say that dad leaves and never comes back. A child may believe that problem is his/her fault. The child may think he/she caused the divorce, or it was their fault that mom and dad didn't stay together. Maybe the child thinks he/she was too much trouble.

That's absolutely, totally untrue; but sometimes children believe and bury these lies. And, the abandonment hurts deeply, sometimes to the point of being toxic.

If there was abuse – verbal, physical, sexual, spiritual – whatever kind of abuse there might have been, a child will automatically assume it was his/her fault. In any violation case where boundaries are crossed, the child can unconsciously think, "Something is wrong with me. This is my fault. Maybe I deserved it." And, usually there are toxic emotions.

It may be that you grew up where there was a lot of control, where mom or dad was like a dictator and crossed personal boundaries in the family life. You must take the responsibility for your own insecurities and unmet needs, or you can carry them throughout your life and place false expectations or difficult demands on someone else to meet those needs. The strategies used to get needs met can then become co-dependent behavior, which is unhealthy. They can also become dangerous wound inducers to others.

NEEDY PEOPLE

Some single people think that marriage is the hope of their lives, and that finding a mate will make them whole and meet their needs. That one is funny to me! After reading this book, it should make you smile too! If you ever hear someone make a comment like that, you'd better look at the person and say, "Honey, you'd better get whole first!"

Because of unmet needs and the shame that comes because of them, we cross boundaries and expect the men or women in our lives, our children, our girlfriends or boyfriends, the church, or our jobs to meet needs that can't possibly be met by any human being. Only God can meet those needs. We must allow God to heal us so that we don't have to try and get something met in the emotions that only God can meet. Only then can we be sound and whole.

Without dealing with personal neediness that comes from the past, people can continue to hide within their jobs or behind their ministries. Some will go deeper into addiction, or will pull the covers of their emotional outbursts up a little higher and think it's okay.

A WORD OF ENCOURAGEMENT

Maybe your children have already grown up, and you're just now realizing some things that you, as a parent, had trouble with. Maybe you're seeing that your inner shame and emotional patterns produced some trouble within your family. If so, you don't have to torture yourself if you lacked in some area. **It's never too late to heal yourself and your relationships.**

Even if your kids have already moved out of the house, you can do a work with God in your own heart and life.

Shame is also a spirit, and when you address it in the natural and in the spirit, it can be broken. Even if your children live far away and have families of their own, if you do the spiritual and emotional work, it will help to prepare a way for them and your children's children to not have to face some of the very same painful emotional issues that you had to face. If you feel like you've failed, or you now see how your emotional life affected your family, then now is the time to let God bring a strong healing.

Personally, if there is something I can do to make my relationship with God, myself, my peers, and my family better, I want to do it. By working on myself today, and allowing my emotions to be released and healed, I am establishing a healthy foundation for the future of my children and my children's children.

I want my generation and the generations that follow me to be healed from shame and the pain that creates dysfunction in families. I want to create a place where the people in my home can be real and healthy. I don't want them to develop dependent behaviors to get their needs met. I want them to be able to be true to themselves. I don't want anyone to have to wear a mask or hide behind a cover. I want all types of healing and deliverance to be active in my home. Not just the Word of God, prayer, and dealing with the devil; but a clear, working knowledge of emotional health and of how to have a balanced family life, free from dysfunctional and codependent behavior.

It's all by the grace of God. I know that I'm not perfect; but I believe that by God's grace, my family can have their emotional love tanks full and brimming. If there's something I can do to help it, then I want to do it.

Every amount of work that we do will set someone free.

Remember, it's never too late. And it's never too late to allow God to give you a season of self-awareness and discovery. Do you know why? Because as Christians, everything we do, in every part of our lives affects the spiritual world. If a handful of Christians will just start examining themselves and allow God to heal them and work deep within them, it will have a positive effect in the spirit world and prepare a way for others to do their work. **What you do is very important.** Every area of your life counts!

I couldn't agree more with the authors of <u>Secrets of Your Family Tree</u> when they state, *"The family today faces challenges and threats unlike those any previous generation experienced. Shocking divorce statistics, rising numbers of incest victims, surging increases in incidents of abuse, and the presence of multitudes of single adults afraid to marry (or remarry) after observing the pain around them – all are symptomatic of a society responding to, and inundated with, trauma."* [5]

I hope that even in reading this book, you and I are creating a way for a new dimension of healing, a new anointing to break these yokes quickly and easily, and a new level of holiness to come to God's people, and to our families and nation. Let's take it seriously and get as much knowledge and healing as we can. The time is now!

Chapter 12

COVER-UPS:
ADDICTIONS

Although the pain and the shame may sound tough to overcome, sometimes the most difficult to confront are the masks that we wear to conceal the wounds. Much like Adam and Eve, we unconsciously and unintentionally have sewn our covers – our human, man-made fig leaves – together to hide the shame, because shame thrives in darkness and secrecy. It intends to hide and stay hidden, while the pain and unfinished business drives from within continually, so that we will divert its uncomfortableness.

Really, people will do almost anything to hide from pain and also to prevent potential pain. They will control, strategize, manipulate, reason, and argue. Logical people will behave illogically. Weak people will become strong. Gracious people will become rude. People will do anything in order to get their way so they will feel secure and protected. Of course, there is no lasting security or protection available through control or any other cover. So, pain drives people to feel they always need to do more, even though they know deep inside that they cannot do enough. Even if the pain is low-grade and only occurs in cycles, at times there is no rest and no peace. Instead there is a constant, relentless drive that can consume entire lives if there isn't recognition of and freedom from the insidious patterns.

Our "fig leaves" consist of covers through addictions, performances, compulsions, and personality masks that we use to shelter ourselves so others can't see who we really are.

It is exhausting to carry family secrets and unfinished business in the heart. Any solution, no matter how temporary or unhealthy, is usually acceptable in the mind of the injured. Any type of cover, however subtle, is usually an extreme behavior; and we usually can't see our unhealthy habits unless someone points it out to us. Many times it's hard get rid of the covers until the pain is healed.

Regardless, a cover can be a good indication that some pain may be present. I didn't realize that I had some inner pain until I looked under the depression I was experiencing. Along with this chapter, the next two chapters will reveal some of the various covers we use to veil our pain. Let's uncover some of the masks or compulsions that we use to camouflage and comfort our inner life. If you'll dare to examine your own life, you might begin to see that there are some toxic emotions at the core of your being.

WHAT IS ADDICTION?

Drugs, alcohol, tobacco, and food are just a few of the words associated with addictions, but the subject extends far past those things. Not all addictions are substance-based. Let me interject from the beginning that I am not saying every habit is an addiction. Nor do I mean that under every addictive behavior is a cesspool of emotional trauma and pain.

I only want to present some basic thoughts that can serve as tools that allow you to do some of your own self-discovery. I am not a trained professional, nor do I profess to be an expert in this subject, but out of necessity, I have studied much on the subject. I needed to be equipped to help myself walk in victory, as well as try to help the many hurting Christians that have come to me and shared the depths of the emotional turmoil and disturbing incidents in their pasts – as well as some of the addictive behaviors they are honestly and openly admitting is currently active in their private lives.

An addiction is something we stay dependent upon, other than God, to cover or medicate inner pain; *and* **to get relief from the uncomfortable feelings produced by toxic emotions.** The first consequence of an addiction is emotional numbness. An addiction is something we use regularly, and can be so habitual, yet acceptable, that we don't even realize it may be hindering us from facing emotional pain. Not every addiction is a covering for pain; but most of them are. Some addictions are simply learned behavior patterns that need to be changed. Regardless of the category, there is a central truth: An addiction is a human *doing* rather than a human *being*. An addiction is an attempt to meet a need by *doing* instead of by just *being*. They rely on finding something dependable that you can count on to meet your needs.

Most Christian and secular psychologists say that most addictions have their root in shame. When the shame begins to be addressed, the addictive power loses its strength and purpose, because the shame gets healed, and so do the toxic emotions that are with it.

The roots of addictions are family dysfunction, personal trauma, and an addictive society. Dr. Ted Roberts, in his book, <u>For Men Only</u>, states, *"The elements of addiction are found in human nature, in the desire within all of us to make it through life with the least amount of pain and the highest amount of pleasure possible."* [6]

We don't always see extreme behavior in our lives because usually, we've incorporated the behaviors as part of our being. But others, whether they see it or not are affected by it. If you find that an extreme behavior is present in your life, you will need to go before God and allow the Holy Spirit to help you with the courage to face it. He will meet you in such a beautiful way. You will need to repent from your behavior because if addictions are working in your life, somewhere along the line it has affected the people around you. And, most definitely it has closed God out of an area of your life. Why? Because the truth is, addictions are always self-serving and self-protecting. Let me briefly and simply mention just a few addictive behaviors. There are several that I will not mention (like food, drugs, alcohol) for the sake of space and time. The same would apply for these compulsions as well.

SEXUAL ADDICTION

The statistics on sexual addiction are alarming. Why do you think there's so much sexual addiction in our society, and even in the church? We're not going to go into great detail here, but often specialists say that sexual addiction, many times, has nothing to do with the person liking sexual encounters. There's a deeper reason. What is it? Reasons are varied; but somewhere in the root of the problem are toxic emotions.

Sexual addiction affects both men and women, and carries with it some very strong and specific emotional dynamics. In his book, Dr. Ted Roberts listed the following statistics:

- 81% of all sex addicts were sexually abused as children.
- 42% have been addicted themselves to drugs and/or alcohol.

- 38% have eating disorders.
- 87% have addicts in their families.

The statistics indicate clearly that male/female sexual addiction is so strong it can reach across an entire life span and touch generations of a family. Tens of thousands of Christians are believed to be in the grip of pornography. Those in counseling ministries estimate that one in three Christians have some sort of struggle with pornography or other sexual addiction.

Sexual addictions come from an unmet need deep within a person, which usually originates with the family of origin. People become addicted to this sort of activity because they need, or have an extreme desire to feel wanted or powerful. Perhaps they felt abandoned or unwanted by their parents as a child; so now in their adult lives, this unmet emotional need has become distorted and toxic, and they are left with an insatiable need to feel wanted. Hence, they become addicted to the false pretense of want and desire through sexual addiction. The hunger for power works much the same way through this particular addiction, as it gives an illusive perception of control and dominance. The cycle is vicious and very atrocious.

The addiction manifests; then it's followed by shame and remorse. Even though this addiction is very real and very serious, it becomes a game these people play, a cover used to hide deeper emotional problems. It usually has nothing to do with present relationships, except for the fact that sexual addiction can destroy them.

Sexual addiction seems like harmless play at the beginning; but as with any compulsion, it will crumble away at a personality until it consumes its victim. The inner desire to feel wanted, or to feel in control is **never** met through an addiction. Unmask it; receive healing for empty spaces of your heart, and live the life that God intended for you to have. Heal the shame; fill the spaces. Then there will not be a need to satisfy the pain through this addiction.

The March 2000 issue of <u>Charisma</u> magazine, page 94, quotes Doug Weiss who runs a Christian counseling program in Fort Worth, Texas. He said, *"If you really want to have **REVIVAL** in your church, you will heal the sex addicts, because once they are free from guilt and shame, they are going to want to fulfill their calling and ministry."*

Yes! Let's heal **ALL** the addictive behavior and the toxic emotions that go with them. It takes some long, hard work; but we can do it! Let's have revival!

GAMBLING, MONEY, AND MATERIALISM

Gambling addictions can also destroy an individual and their families. We've all seen and heard about those who are feeling bad, and then gamble to make themselves feel better by winning. When they lose, the feelings intensify and become worse. I could tell many stories about addictions, but they speak for themselves.

Some people are addicted to their credit cards or spending money. This extreme behavior motivates people to buy things that will fill the void in their lives. It's a vicious cycle that can lead to severe financial problems. It doesn't work because it causes more pain, more hardship, and more problems. Haven't you heard people say that money isn't everything? They've discovered that money isn't the answer to the pain and confusion in their lives.

I believe that in the body of Christ, we really need to be careful about what we teach to motivate people about material things. A sign of God's blessing or status with Him isn't in the "things" you acquire, or how much money you have. There are countless men and women in the Scriptures who didn't have expensive, material things, yet were mightily blessed and anointed by God to be a voice in their generation.

Material things or business success doesn't make you a whole person. I believe that God wants to prosper us financially; but the flesh gets so hungry after "things" that people's entire lives become motivated and dictated by success and money. I think it's better that we find and search for God instead of money.

WORKAHOLICS

People can be addicted to their computer or their work. Who are workaholics? They are the ones who have an extreme willingness to spend time and energy on business goals, rather than on themselves or their families. It is work out of balance.

Honestly, I can relate to this particular addiction because through it, I discovered the pain and the fear I was unknowingly covering.

I was an avid workaholic. Sometimes the work of the ministry gets distorted by thinking that being loyal to God means you have to sacrifice yourself unnecessarily. Humorously, if you looked the word up in a dictionary, my picture was there!

Years ago, I submitted to a stress test. On a normal chart, the stress level should be 150. To give you an idea of the pace I ran, my test scored 710!

I talked with someone about the results. We talked about why I was so stressed. We talked about why I kept so busy. When he saw that I was a little relaxed, he asked me why I felt that I *had* to be so busy.

I remember thinking, "Please stop asking me that question."

Why? Because shame wants to hide. I felt something welling up inside of me that was very uncomfortable. Little did I know that fig leaf was being slowly ripped from my life and revealing an area of shame and unhealthy behavior. The man was persistent. Although he was gentle, he had little regard for the feelings of my shame and toxic emotions. He would continue to ask the same question; and week after week I wondered why I continued talking with him.

One monumental day, he had me in the place that he wanted. Without any warning, he leaned right up to my face and asked, "What is hiding behind that mask of busyness that you don't want others to see?"

I remember how close he was to my face when he asked that question. And I remember thinking if he got a fraction closer, I was going to take my fist and punch him out! My shame was touched, and this man – brother in Christ or not – had come into the sheer fabric of it in my heart.

He probably realized that he was about to be slugged, but he fearlessly continued. "What reality are you going to deal with if you slow down and let God be God? What reality will come if you quit trying to do everything in your own strength?"

With all my defenses gone, I said the golden words of truth.

"I have this fearful and empty feeling deep down inside that if I don't stay busy, everything is going to fail."

There. I said it. I had a fear of failure, and a bucket-load of shame about failure – so I worked and worked and worked myself to a frazzle. I was unintentionally camouflaging the core issue of control, of being over-responsible for myself and others, and neglecting my own needs.

I'll never forget what he said. "That's interesting. So you're the center of your world." I'll also never forget the intensity of the feeling of shame that I had inside of me. I didn't know it was shame at the time. But I will never forget how it felt.

As we continued to talk about it, he kept repeating himself. "So what? So what if you fail? What's everyone going to do if Mary Alice falls down? What does it really mean if you fail?"

Now this might not strike a note with you, because you may not struggle with this particular issue. But that day, he dealt with that fear of failure and the shame surrounding that fear. There was a sense of shame within me, a hopelessness, an internal bleeding saying that the world would be over if I failed in the major areas of my life.

Of course, all the religion that I had been taught and believed piled on top of it. Unbalanced teaching puts people under legalism and taps into their shame, driving them to *perform* in the name of God with Bible verses to match. After awhile, these teachings can make people believe if they're not making top dollar, have not climbed the ladder of success, or not found their ministry, they're not good enough for God or His Kingdom, because they don't have His blessing. I thought that if I failed, then I proved I wasn't good enough. And if I had failed, I would have deserved the deep pain that would have been there for me.

Part of the issue was a spiritual generational curse; I prayed and broke it. Part of it I perceived and learned in my childhood; and part of it was mere human nature. Whatever the case, **I now had to learn about, walk out and heal the dysfunctional behavior and toxic emotions that went with the unhealthy, destructive pattern that was being revealed and resolved within me.**

Do you know what I had to do? A part of my healing was to go before that man of God and before my Heavenly Father, and bring that shame into the light. I had to name the shame. In the presence of God, I let go of my ministry and I allowed it to fall. I was trembling and crying, but I went before the Lord and let go of my preaching, my gift, my reputation, my money, my results, all of it, and smashed it to smithereens. Everything died before the Lord. I allowed myself to move into the trapped feelings within me, instead of running away from them. Now was the time of release. I could do it, I could cope. I could win! I felt the unreleased shame in me when I went there, but I knew that I would go through it to the other side if I just wouldn't close up and back out of that feeling.

I can't even describe the release, the darkness, and the pressure that lifted from me when I passed through the shame. It took a few days of feeling strange and a bit uncomfortable, but the light healed it, and I can honestly say that if my ministry crashes tomorrow, it won't be the end of the world for me.

The enemy tried to own me through busywork, lock, stock, and barrel. My gift was ruling me and running me, to the point where I was running myself into the ground. I had no life, no time for what God desired to do for me or bring to me personally. Now, I don't have to live that way anymore, and I'm not ashamed of taking care of myself, meeting my needs, and setting boundaries on where and how other people receive from me.

Of course, some still try to heap shame on me by commenting, "Mary Alice, your ministry is not progressing enough; you need to do something." I don't respond anymore because I'm not driven by those inner compulsions and unsettled areas anymore.

The day that my self-worth through work died on the altar of the Lord, He in return worked a very deep peace and acceptance into the core of my being. He totally healed my shame in that area and replaced it with His mercy and grace. Now I can be real and relaxed!

Some of the things we do may fail. Welcome to life! Some things don't work; but that doesn't mean we have to internalize failure into our being and or allow it to sabotage our well-being as a person.

Today I'm a hard worker; but I'm not a workaholic. I am detaching from the dysfunctional system that taught me the shame of failure and I have healed the pain of the needs that weren't met in the early stages of my life, that drove my work to be an idol. The pressure from others won't influence me anymore. I realize that my entire self-worth is tied up in what Jesus Christ did for me on the cross – and that's all I need. That's all I desire.

TELEVISION

People are addicted to television. You may be moaning, "Don't start on that. I only watch Christian stations."

Okay. But why is it that every time you come home, you have to turn the television on? Why can't you go to sleep without listening to the television, or the radio, or the stereo? Why do you always have to have it going in the background? It's almost like people are afraid of what they would discover in the silence. I meet a lot of people who are addicted to television.

SPORTS AND EXERCISE

Some are addicted to sports and exercise. You're probably laughing, wishing you could be a little more extreme in the area of exercise! But honestly, this addiction is so self-centered. We need the balance in taking care of our bodies; but making our bodies a god is an extreme behavior.

The area of sports speaks for itself. We've all heard of people showing extreme emotion during games, but none for God and little for their families. Some put their lives or families in debt to buy tickets for sporting events. I heard of a grown man who cried at the threat of his favorite college football team not playing games in his city anymore. That is an extreme behavior towards sports.

RELATIONSHIPS

For example, a relationship can become addictive. Maybe someone makes you feel good, or takes you away from the pain you've experienced. Once the good feelings wear off, new conflict may begin. When we refuse to deal with pain, we only take action to cover it. The cover doesn't heal it; it only medicates it. Sooner or later there will be another circumstance, another person, or another time when the pain will manifest again. This cycle continues until the pain is dealt with, or healed.

CHURCH

The last area of addiction that I'm going to boldly talk about is a relatively untouched one; but a very needed one. Brace yourself: Some people are addicted to **church and ministry.**

As a former pastor, I learned this well. I wanted people to come to church; but not to the point of physical and emotional unhealthiness for themselves or their families. I did my best to give them teaching that would lead them to God and His grace, not to me and a religious legalism.

In our generation, we keep the church active, filling each day with a multitude of activities because there are a multitude of needs and a variety of people. The problem comes when as leaders, we expect every family to be at *every* thing! It's unhealthy to even expect your leaders to be at *every* function! Where's the nurturing time left for their families or for their own personal lives? Do you expect them to be at every function that lasts until late in the evening, and then get up before dawn to spend coherent time with God? Aside from all that, do you still expect them to be at work by eight o'clock, five days a week, to carry on throughout an exhausting day, making accurate decisions? If so, that expectation is dysfunctional and unhealthy *for everyone.*

As a pastor, I had to learn to take my expectations off of people. After much self-discovery and some emotional work, **without realizing it, I found that some of my expectations upon them came from my own personal issues.** Adam blamed Eve out of his own issues. Now, you may not be blaming anyone, but you can put unintentional pressure on those around you. Certainly, they have church jobs to do, ministry positions to fill, and growth to attain as believers. But **as a leader, you must take the responsibility to clarify and keep intact emotional boundaries between the people and your personal issues which place an unhealthy demand upon them, and create a dysfunctional environment in the church.** That can't be done if you have no clue where you, yourself are unhealthy.

Our Christianity was birthed from Jewish roots. Whether you like to admit it or not, it's true. The Jews, the first race of people to know and recognize Jehovah, received an original church pattern from the Lord. The Sabbath is very holy and the first portion of it is given to the Lord through every aspect of their lives. But the second half of the Sabbath is spent nurturing and bonding with their families, praising God for the blessing to have one.

I'm not telling you to take up the Jewish faith. I'm simply saying that as Christians, we need to reconsider the areas that we've ignored, especially those which fall under the heading of "ministry work." It's not always an easy balance to find, but we must find it!

There are also people who get their self-worth by what they *do* in the church. Instead of attending church through a loving relationship with God, some show up due to a "performance orientation" inner drive that feeds their self-esteem, their need for approval, and security. They think they're in good standing because they're doing what the pastor wants them to do, or what the latest teaching in the Christian magazines taught them to do. **I am for obedience and new revelation, but I feel we need to do some serious examination of how everything relates to our private inner life and motivations.**

Some people use church attendance as an excuse not to nurture their families. It's a religious mask. When you use the church as an excuse to ignore or be rude and inconsiderate to others, you've missed the whole point of Christianity. All you have is religion.

I've seen others who take abusive, cruel, rude, dishonest, and disrespectful treatment from the leadership and remain in the church, afraid their destiny with God will be aborted if they leave. That's not to mention here the issues surrounding shaming tactics used to get people to give financially.

I've seen some members who take every word from the leadership or others as the literal Word of God, and base their entire lives around it whether it agrees with their personal convictions and values or not. Some even leave their mates and their families over it. That is **spiritual abuse.**

Of course your pastor wants you to come to church! Every accountable and integral pastor wants you to get all from God that you can. **But you must find your pattern of peace, first with God, and then with yourself and your family.**

Then there are those who never come to church, or who only appear every two months when there's a special speaker! These people have no commitment to their church community.

If you are one of these people, what are you hiding? Why won't you fellowship with the brothers and the sisters? Is there something you don't want us to find out? Many times when there are painful issues inside of us, we don't want them revealed. In an environment of love, security, and anointing, those wounds can't hide and they'll surface. The rage, injustice, rebellion, or withdrawal you may experience after being in a church atmosphere may be issues that have been hidden deep within you. God is revealing those areas to you. He wants you to feel them. But because the feelings are so uncomfortable, many choose to stay home and stay away from it. Why? Because those feelings are painful, turbulent, and easier to ignore and medicate with an excuse or cover.

It's interesting to point out that when these painful issues are healed, they then can become a very strong area of ministry the person has to others. Remember, don't ever stop because of the pain. There is a hidden treasure under there, waiting to be released!

It would be impossible to cover every church scenario here. There are many! As I close this section, I want to mention that the relationship between the ministers and congregations must all strive to become mutual. **That means that respect, care, nurturing, and understanding is directed and received in equal amounts by all parties.** Church members can put false and projected expectations on leaders as well. I have witnessed believers who are very judgmental and inconsiderate of a leader's personal financial business life without knowing any details. They feel entitled to give their opinions and influence others just because they tithe or have a position. We all must endeavor to grow and change, and all learn how to set proper, healthy boundaries.

Although church community and attendance is important, in your cycle of emotional healthiness and priorities, believe it or not, church activity **is not** within the inner circle. Here's what I'm talking about.

LET'S TAKE A TEST

To help keep our lives in perspective, what is the circle of wholeness? If you listed your areas of priorities, how would they rate? It's a fun exercise, because when we take the time to evaluate our priorities, we discover where we might be out-of-balance. Addictions and compulsions show clearly when we list the things and people in the order of importance to our lives.

To begin, draw a circle. In that circle, write what is the most important to you. Now, draw a larger circle around that, and list the next thing that is important. Continue until you've drawn seven circles, and listed in sequential order what is important to you. You may have several things in the same circle. That's okay. The key to this is in your honesty. No one has to see what you've written unless you choose. This is a test that will certainly reveal where your life may be unbalanced.

HERE ARE THE ANSWERS

Before I give the answers, please understand that sometimes, each one of these circles might need to be juggled in order to give help in another area. **Although they are correct in your foundational priorities,** don't be overly rigid with it when an emergency arises, or if the church is having a special meeting that you can clear your work schedule for. I'm not giving you these areas of priorities as another excuse for extreme behavior!

In the core of the inner circle should be **you** and **God.** God is your first priority; and as we've discussed, you must take care of yourself so that other circumstances and situations can be clearly and accurately evaluated.

If you're married, the next circle of priority should be your **spouse.** Your mate is bone of your bone, flesh of your flesh. Every situation of your spouse's life should be highly important to you, and evaluated within the boundaries of your own life.

The next circle should contain your **children that still live at home.** Everything that your children will encounter in life finds its foundation in the home. After the family life chapter, you should realize your God-given responsibility to the children in your home.

The next circle would contain your **children that are grown.** As adults, you must allow them to make decisions on their own. Your responsibility to them is important, but limited. They will still need guidance, consultation, and encouragement as they begin to set their adult lives in order.

After that circle, **work** should fill the next place. The Bible clearly states in 1 Timothy 5:8, that if anyone doesn't provide for, or work to take care of his own, the person is worse than someone who doesn't believe in God. It's important, especially for workaholics to understand that while the job is important, it is designed to aide your family. It was never designed to take the place of your family or your other priorities.

Close, intimate friends should fill the next space. We've already discussed that relationships are very important in our journey to become open, honest, and accountable. Good relationships, sent by God, help to bring out the best in us.

The last circle should contain **church** activities. Church is very important in the circle of wholeness, and should have a place in your circle of priorities. It adds to your knowledge of God, and helps you to understand how to excel in the other priorities of your life. Christians sometimes get God and church confused and blended together. While it is true that there is nothing like the wonderful atmosphere of corporate anointing, worship, and fellowship, we must understand that if every church closed today, God would still be with you.

In addition to addictions, there are also behavior compulsions. While most of these are also a cover-up for pain, some are just uncontrolled emotions that need correcting and training. Let's talk about them, and then we'll discuss the attitudes that fashion as cover-ups as well. When we see the entire picture, we'll build up to the cure.

Chapter 13

COVER-UPS:
UNCONTROLLED EMOTIONS

Behavior compulsions are really uncontrolled emotions that a lot of people don't realize they have. They can be emotions that are unrestrained inside of you, or they can be emotions that are expressed at home in explosive episodes when no one else sees. Most of the time, these extreme behaviors signal an internal problem. If addiction is not used as a cover-up, you'll usually find an unbalanced behavior trying to do the job. I have mentioned just a few in this chapter.

HATRED

Hatred can become an emotion out of control when someone won't deal with pain or shame inside of them. This kind of person uses hatred as something he/she likes to play with. In fact, these people are very mean, sometimes abusive, and they love to play manipulative games. Because of their own inward hurt, they like to see other people suffer, thinking it brings them some sort of personal recompense.

People use hatred through sarcasm, through childish manipulation, and mind games. For them it's normal, natural behavior because it's a part of the way they are.

I've seen Christians that are inwardly waiting anxiously for someone else to fail so that they can get a position. I've seen the ones, who because of their own emotional turmoil, betray some one else and kick others while they are down, all to put themselves up. These people may not release hate or attack openly, but you can see it in their eyes. This behavior is far from the heart of God, and very unscriptural.

Hatred is a terrible thing. There are man-hating demeanors that women have. There are women-hating demeanors that men have. Demonic spirits love to grab hold and work with these behaviors, wrecking havoc and causing hurt and hardship.

ARROGANCE

Arrogance usually shows a hardened heart. It can develop as a learned behavior; but most of the time, it's hiding pain and shame. Actually, it would be a natural opposite to shame. After all, if you don't want to feel bad about something, just choose the other side – be proud. Make yourself or something about yourself big and important. This comes in many styles.

Some people act arrogant and prideful because of their race or culture. It's healthy to be proud of who you are and where you came from; but it's an extreme to be rudely arrogant about it. Those who behave this way may be hiding shame from the way their race or culture has been treated in the past, or is treated presently. Any racial militant group, no matter the color, can be exemplifying extreme behavior that may have its core in pain and shame.

Religion that becomes a taskmaster finds its base in arrogance. God doesn't want you to have a "religion" for Him. He wants you to have a "relationship" with Him through Jesus Christ. But religious people place laws and expectations on everyone and everything, acting "holier than thou." All of these arrogant, judgmental expectations hold you at bay, because who can live up to them?

Webster's II New Riverside Dictionary defines arrogant as "overbearing, self-important, haughty, superior, insolent, lofty, lordly." The definition speaks for itself.

Arrogance is an exaggerated sense of yourself. You become your own idol of importance. I guess you can call it a form of self-worship. Arrogance is a cover-up that makes people think that they're better than others, so they become judgmental, patronizing, self-righteous, and critical.

I have had to deal with this kind of behavior in my life.

Thank God, I had a mentor who became a tormentor in my face! Thank God she did so I could pull off those fig leaves! It is really good to deal with things in our lives!

I would tell her my thoughts about people and situations, and how I acted, and she'd sarcastically but honestly say, "That's a really pure way for a leader. You know, you carry an attitude of arrogance."

Then she'd straightforwardly, but gently say, "You're the proudest of them all."

She would say those things to help me see the issues inside of me. Boy, how she did! Remember, shame likes to hide; but when it's threatened, the shame and all its cover-up tactics will manifest!

She made me so mad sometimes that I never wanted to see her again, much less talk to her. But I had to trust her. She provided a safe, mature environment for me, and I wanted desperately to be healed and whole, and to become a leader who operates with integrity and a balance of power.

She laughs about it all now and says, "You were one of the most resilient people that I've ever had to train. You've got such a strong mind and will. It was like arm-wrestling. I'd almost get you down and you'd pop back up!" With the call of God on my life, there were mental and emotional issues I had to settle; strong wrestlings with God, strong attacks from the devil, and fortified areas of my soul that needed to be tamed or healed. But God was there through it all. Wow! What a miracle! He not only walked with me, but led me through it and healed me.

The Bible is full of verses that speak of how God feels about prideful or hardened hearts. Proverbs 8:13 says,

"The fear of the Lord is to hate evil: pride and arrogancy. ..."

Proverbs 11:2 speaks of the cycle of shame and the cover of arrogancy. It says,

"When pride cometh, then cometh shame. ..."

The good news is that you don't have to wear a mask of arrogance to appear that you are worth something. In Psalm 51:10, David cried to the Lord and prayed,

"Create in me a clean heart, O God; and renew a right spirit within me."

If your heart is hardened, God can make it soft and tender once again. If you'll ask, God can and will create a new, clean heart inside of you.

SELF-ABSORPTION

This cover is related to arrogance and pride, though slightly different. It's not really an exaggerated emotion, but instead, is a clear presentation of insecurity. It's an exaggerated cover of self-importance or self-absorption. It's just plain and intense selfishness.

People who portray this behavior are always calling attention to themselves and their own issues. They over-exaggerate in the way they dress, many times being far too seductive; or they may demonstrate behavior that attracts inappropriate sexual attention. They act very proud of their behavior, when honestly, they are embarrassed by it.

Self-absorbed individuals may show-off or exaggerate the way they live; the authority they carry on the job; even with who they know. Most of the time, they are very self-serving. This type can be master "name-droppers." They even over-exaggerate their gifts and callings in the ministry, and can't compliment others or even acknowledge that other people exist or have anything going on in their lives.

As a Christian, have you ever met a person who is constantly talking about his/her gift or anointing? It's usually a screen for insecurity and low self-worth. These types of people believe if they can convince others that they possess something of importance, then others will accept them. It's one thing to speak of what you are called by God to do. But it's quite another to incessantly talk about the way God uses you, or to constantly talk about the so-and-so who prophesied how great your ministry will be, or who you know in the ministry circles.

Self-absorbed people literally thrive off the praise and adoration of others. If you know a Christian like that, I'd venture to say the person is more concerned with his/her gift than with loving and caring for people. This behavior that manifests through a Christian is a cheap imitation for the true love of Christ to a hurting and hungry world.

Remember, we are very important to God. In fact, we are of such value to Him that there's no way I could describe it all in this book. Allow Him to heal the areas that you are looking for others to heal, and needs you are looking for others to meet. There's an old adage that says, "It matters not if the world has heard, or approves, or understands. The only applause we're meant to seek is that of the nail-scarred hands." When the shame is healed, it doesn't matter if others accept you or reject you. Oh, you may feel a few twinges of the old feelings later, but the victory of the healing is that you don't live under the domination of them anymore.

RAGE

We've already discussed that anger is an emotion, and within its proper boundaries, is acceptable and needed. In the Old Testament alone, the Bible records 375 times when God got angry. Anger tells us when we have been violated. But rage is anger out of control.

When rage happens, it's not only the sense of being violated, but the feeling goes deeper and touches the sense of shame buried within a person, thus making the emotion toxic.

Rage is a more aggressive tactic to cover shame, because the raging person acutely senses that someone is threatening him/her. What the rage-filled person is really saying is, "Don't get closer to me or I'll attack." Most of the time, they *do* attack with physical or verbal abuse.

Road rage is a very prevalent illness in our culture, and sometimes death has been the result of it. People behind the wheel who react in road rage are saying the very same thing, "Don't get any closer. You're getting too close, you're in my space. If you get closer, I'll make you pay for it." The boundary issue has blown out of proportion for a rager, and any small thing can set them off.

When people come to me with the problem of rage, I always try to help them locate the deeper issues by asking, "What is it that makes you feel so threatened?" Or, what is it that makes you feel so agitated, sensitive, and upset? We must understand that if we don't know how to get rid of the shame, we can't get rid of the rage. Rage is not normal. It's over-reacting to a given situation or to a person.

Some women fly into a rage when it comes to men, because other men have shamed them and vice versa. Some go into a rage with their parents because somewhere in their past, the parents humiliated them. A mother or father might go into a rage when a child doesn't obey immediately because she/he feels inadequate as a parent. Some employers go into a rage when an employee makes a mistake, because the employer has been criticized and shamed by others.

Rage works hard to keep people from getting close to the rager. Sometimes rage goes so far as abuse, and it's very sad. Abusive people are filled with shame. Abused people are filled with shame. So you can see, shame begets shame.

I have only listed a few of the extreme emotional responses that are evident when someone is carrying toxic shame and emotions. The next area I want to discuss could stand on its own as a book – the dysfunctional, codependent behavior roles assumed in family life to cope with the emotional issues there.

Chapter 14

COVER-UPS:
BEHAVIOR ROLES

Each individual family unit has adopted several ways in which to cope with the emotional equilibrium in the family. Somewhere in the family dynamics, needs are met, and emotional issues are dealt with either in a healthy or unhealthy way. Each family has its own personality or a pattern it uses to express itself to those outside, the way it conducts its business within, and the hierarchy of values it establishes for all who belong.

Each child in the family probably responded and related differently based on their individual personality, needs, and treatment. Usually to cope with all the dynamics of family life, each person takes on a particular role, and then uses that role to meet their needs or establish their identity. If life is too hard, the child cultivates the role just to survive emotionally.

You may find yourself resisting and even denying the dysfunctional roles described here. Sometimes if the family of origin had a high degree of this kind of relating, it can be difficult or painful to closely explore the inner structures and workings of the family life. Remember, because of the fallen nature of all parents and children, all families are flawed and therefore dysfunctional to a certain degree.

As each person takes their place, the roles become *codependent* on each other, and blend together in a combination that makes up the life of the family. They need each other functioning in their roles to meet certain needs. Therefore, they become dependent upon each other, and uniquely and dysfunctionally tied. When the children grow up, they carry the roles and the rules into their adult relationships and try to make those work. Hence we have an emotional mess in the family life of America today.

God wants you to locate which role you fulfilled and why you did. He wants you to expose all the rules that were there and the needs in your life that were not met because of how you were treated and how the family functioned – dysfunctionally. The healing that can come by gaining knowledge in this area, and then by healing the shame and toxic feelings that you carry from the inner life of your original family is great. So is learning proper and healthy ways to relate, even though it may be difficult to understand and work if you never got some things from your parents and family life. God can put knowledgeable people in your path to help you heal, as well as teach you the proper ways to get your needs met and meet the needs of others in your current family.

I am deeply convinced that the church needs to stop shunning, ignoring, and mocking the conceptual truths found in both the thorough study *and* the working knowledge of areas regarding dysfunction and emotional health.

People coming into the present church as new believers have had a hard life. They need to be saved; but they also deserve the chance to understand themselves, and heal their inner life and relationships. More than any other time in history, lifelong believers are more mature in spiritual things; but in many cases lack emotional and relational soundness.

I am not promoting that churches now become "psychologically" based, or make this the "new direction."

However, the churches that I have been exposed to who are actively teaching and incorporating these concepts in the local body, are seeing tremendous and powerful results in the believer's life and family. I am still learning about emotional health on a daily basis, and my prayer is that you will pursue this as well, as the Lord leads you and gives you grace to do so.

One last thought before we look at these roles. As we go into this, please be sure that you have a non-judgmental heart toward yourself and others. You are bound to see someone here, so let's look with loving, non-judgmental, non-critical eyes!

THE ENABLER / CARETAKER

To be an enabler or a rescuer, it means that you're dependent for your self-worth and your needs being met by what you do for others. The enabler, caretaker, or rescuer is a dependent behavior pattern that you've developed over your life because of what you've been exposed to, what you learned at home, or how you feel on the inside. Some people have developed this cover to emotionally survive a chaotic family life through this role. Personally, at times I've been a classic caretaker and unknowingly, I did it to make myself feel better and dysfunctionally meet my needs. When I couldn't take care of someone, I would get uncomfortable and restless. People really hated it when I would cross over into their boundaries because of my inward need to enable them.

I used to get an emotional pay off by overly nurturing friends, my church, and whoever else crossed my life. Then I would end up depressed, sick in bed, my own needs unmet, and bitter because of it! Whose fault was it? Mine.

Once you get peace in your soul, you don't have to take care of everyone, solve everything for everyone, or nurture anything that comes around you. Because of that peace, now I don't get an emotional need met, or cover my wounds by taking anyone's cares, or running to their rescue all the time. I thank God for the light of the Holy Spirit. And I am sure my intimates are glad about it as well!

Sometimes the role of the enabler can be a good role. But if it's not constantly in check, the behavior becomes destructive. Why? Because an enabler tries to solve everyone else's dilemma at their own expense. They don't want to look at themselves. The busier they stay, the less they have to think about their own situation. Enablers try to solve situations and "become the answer" in their family life, in their church life, in the workplace – the list goes on and on. It can certainly drain you when you're busy taking care of everybody else all the time, and making no time to care for yourself.

THE HERO / PERFECTIONIST

Most behaviors are roles that people have learned or take upon themselves. As I've just stated, some of these roles can be good in their beginnings; but they become conduct that can be destructive.

The hero role is another behavioral cover-up. This behavior pattern tries to be perfect all the time. You could call them perfectionists.

Perfectionism and excellence are two different things. Excellence comes from the character of a person. Excellence is simply "being." Excellence does what it right and what is integral in any situation.

Perfectionism is always "doing," trying to make sure that everything is perfect enough so the person will look good, or so that their world won't be rocked. These people think they're only valued for what they do. They evaluate others on what others *do*. This behavioral pattern is never pleased with themselves or others. Why? Because the core of its root is fear.

The hero, or perfectionist, unconsciously thinks if things aren't perfect, then their personal flaws will be revealed. They think if they make a mistake, if the cover is let down, then someone might not like them. So they're always in a frenzy, always driven, and nit-picking. Their personality has to have everything in place; every hair, every relationship, every church member, every word, every detail, every number – everything has to be perfect!

If one thing goes wrong – watch out! Everyone around them walks on egg shells, especially if they're working on a project that a perfectionist is overseeing! The hero, or perfectionist, has this illusion that if everything is perfect enough, all their problems will go away and there will be peace. They avoid new activities because they're afraid they might do it wrong. If they can keep from making a mistake, it holds shame at bay. It's a cover-up and it's never fulfilling. In fact, *everyone* suffers around them.

THE SCAPEGOAT

This behavioral pattern can find its root in rebellion. Maybe in the scapegoat's family, they were always the black sheep. Maybe they didn't do things like everyone else; so it marked them inside to think they are the problem, and that everyone was always judging or blaming them.

Some people rebel and react because they don't want a situation to get too close to them. They've been very hurt in the past, and perhaps labeled all kinds of names. Remember, shame doesn't like to be located, so a scapegoat behavior will use the cover of rebellion to keep someone away from them.

The sad fact about shame is that it deceives a person into thinking he/she is a bad person and will never be good enough. The scapegoat has believed that lie, and hides the shame of it by rebelling against the family's problems with erratic behavior. They also can become a constant "stressor" by creating chaos that everyone else has to consistently appease in some way.

THE LOST CHILD

Many people suffer with this behavioral cover. Remember that all of these cover-ups can be shielding the core of shame, with its loneliness and hurt inside of a person.

The lost child is a master at withdrawing. There can be several factors in the family or the church that trigger this cover. It could be the fear of abandonment, the fear of receiving another hurt, or perhaps the fear of failure. Whatever the reason, the lost child shrinks when situations become uncomfortable or unbearable for them.

Contact with another person or a certain situation can be too painful to handle; and the lost child feels, if I stay there, it will increase my pain or shame. So they withdraw, become passive, or run. Their withdrawal causes confusion and hurt that can break relationships.

Sometimes this behavior flares up in stressful or painful situations; or it flares up when someone else is in pain. The lost child also becomes passive when direct confrontation comes, because healthy confrontation is threatening to them. They withdraw and become quiet, because they're afraid of what others might think of them and afraid they will be emotionally crushed. They are embarrassed by attention because they feel different and out of place.

If you have toxic shame, sometimes withdrawal is the easiest way out because it seems sinister if someone gets too close. If you don't understand why you act the way you do and that shame is what you are feeling, then the thought of confrontation becomes unbearable. You'll do almost anything to avoid it.

The lost child behavior pulls itself into a shell, withdraws, and isolates themselves from meaningful relationships. It's very sad, because many times this person really wants to have a relationship with the person they've withdrawn from. But they can't seem to break through their behavior, because the shame and the pain from unmet needs is not healed within them.

I've known other ministers who have resorted to the expression of a lost child behavior pattern. In the past, they've been hurt by flaky Christians. Because of their unhealed insecurities, they would only get so close to the people, and then they would withdraw because of fear that the people wouldn't respect them.

Shamed by their weaknesses, they choose to be the professional pastor who just smiles, comes in and out, and keeps a distance from the people.

There is a place for a divine order, rules, respect of leadership, and boundaries in church life; but don't set them up to protect the "lost child" within you. Like the others, this behavior can become a weakness. The Bible is full of scriptures that speak of weaknesses, how we are made strong in them, and how to stand with others through them.

In the Hall of Faith, we can read where the greatest of leaders were made strong through their weaknesses (Hebrews 11:34). But one of the strongest verses in the New Testament gives the secret to humility and strength. The Apostle Paul wrote it in 2 Corinthians 12:10. I'm quoting the Amplified Version. He said,

"So for the sake of Christ, I am well pleased and take pleasure in infirmities, insults, hardships, persecutions, perplexities, and distresses; for when I am weak [in human strength], then am I [truly] strong (able, powerful in divine strength)."

The secret is to enjoy your life, enjoy what God has given you, and learn to enjoy the people He has placed you with, in spite of what they do as a result of their weaknesses. We all have insecurities, but don't withdraw to protect yourself. **God is with you more than you know.** If you refuse to be insecure, God will protect you. Let God be God and allow Him to be the strength in the areas you may fall short.

THE MASCOT

The mascot role is usually the class clown. It's usually individuals who absolutely make you weary of their comedy act, or who always responds with jokes, silliness, or rowdy reactions. Humor is a delightful attribute to any personality, and a merry heart does good like a medicine; but when it's in the extreme through the mascot behavior, it makes one look childish.

Why would you have to be the class clown? Why would you have to be the center of attention all the time? Maybe as a child, your parents weren't available for you. To make up for that loss, cover the void, and meet the need, the practical joker takes the center stage.

THE MARTYR

The name of this role is almost self-explanatory! This is a very negative cover that always believes the worst to be their lot in life. Whenever there's a problem, the martyr immediately takes the blame and remorses over it. Why? Because the martyr has resigned that if the cause of a problem is examined, they will be "the one;" so they shield the pain with self-pity and melancholy.

The number one sign of a martyr behavior is depression. They have mastered the pity party and made everyone miserable.

If this person doesn't take the blame, they project blame. Remember that many times, depression is repressed anger. In Luke 15:28, we can read where the brother of the prodigal son was so angry at his brother's return, that he regressed into a martyr behavior. He refused to go into the celebration party for this brother, and his father had to plead with him to join them. What was that? It was a pity party of repressed anger, jealousy, and depression.

Shame makes people feel they are cheated in life, that they will never be acceptable, and that they are doomed to fail. Sometimes we've thought these extremes were just someone's personality; but that's not always true. These are real behavioral patterns that are designed to divert inward pain and shame, and block the self-discovery.

A victim mentality is related to the martyr. A victim is someone who is harmed by another person, intentionally or unintentionally. It's someone who suffers or is taken advantage of. A victim has a "poor me" attitude as well, usually from someone else's offenses. They are always blaming someone else for the condition they're in. I've seen some who fell apart over a trying situation; and others who have been in much worse conditions and came out better. It all has to do with what's inside the person and what they choose to do with what life hands them.

There is a direct relationship between accepting responsibility for your own happiness and the rewards you will reap. No one else has the power to make you happy or unhappy. You are the one who decides.

Unfortunately, victims can't face the truth, can't face facts, or take responsibility for their own actions, because the victim mentality has become a way of life.

Victims play on a deep sense of helplessness and powerlessness. They thrive on passivity, thinking they have no power to change. They think they'll never have anything unless someone else decides to give it to them.

I want you to ask yourself this question: How much time do I spend on doing something to better my situation? Choose to be a victor and not a victim.

GO AFTER WHAT IS YOURS!

Perhaps you've recognized yourself in some dysfunctional roles, and although it may be shocking to realize it, it's really a very good thing. Don't just sit there and sulk about it, or degrade yourself because of it. Don't go into despondency. Don't ignore it either. Instead, realize that now you have a responsibility to change it. Ask the Holy Spirit to shine more light on it, and prepare yourself for intimacy with the Lord. Talk to close friends that provide a safe environment for you, tell them what you've discovered, and let them speak to you about what they see and know. If the pain becomes too unbearable or shocking as the lid is lifted and light comes in, visit a qualified minister, counselor, or therapist who can help you. There are many good ones available. Going to the roots of your inner life through self-discovery will only better you and those around you. You have a reason to be very optimistic about the future! Above all, continue and pursue until wholeness has its place within you.

I also want to encourage you to find ways to teach yourself some of the things you didn't get in your home life. After all, as a father, how do you emotionally connect with your wife and children if you never had a feelings-level relationship with your own father? If all you knew as a child was sexual abuse, how can you make a positive sexual adjustment in marriage? If you have never seen communication modeled, it's hard to know what "normal" is.

To learn what "normal" is, there are many sources that can help educate or teach you how to manage some of these issues. You need to do some of your own studying from classes, books, TV specials, and the Scriptures. I have included a reading suggestion list at the end of this book. Read these books, pass this one and others to friends, and start talking about what you are learning. Get new information for yourself – don't let your wife, husband, or friend do it! Educate yourself because some of the advice you get is critical for your healing and recovery.

It is great that it's a new day, and we are getting all we need to heal toxic emotions, and to become mature, healthy followers of Christ. It's hard work, but it's worth every second. **Go for it!**

Chapter 15

COVER-UPS:
ATTITUDES

So far, we've discussed three areas that give an illusion of protection from hurt, a false method of properly meeting needs, and a covering for shame. By exposing the compulsions of addictions, uncontrolled emotions, and role-playing, it might have opened your eyes to some things in your own life.

Attitudes are the fourth area that can become master cover-up strategies for what's inside us. Extreme dispositions and opinions weave a very deceptive net, and can be used unintentionally as a disguise to cover pain and shame.

I have found through working with others and through my own self-discovery, that these approaches – addictions, uncontrolled emotions, behavior roles, and attitudes – can become well-developed reactions and unconscious excuses for not dealing with our own heart issues. Frankly, I believe that the temperaments we are about to discuss are some of the largest, most destructive compulsions that we have to face.

DENIAL

"Then David's anger was greatly kindled against the man, and he said to Nathan, As the Lord lives, the man who has done this is a son [worthy] of death.

"He shall restore the lamb fourfold, because he did this thing and had no pity.

"Then Nathan said to David, You are the man! Thus says the Lord, the God of Israel: I anointed you king of Israel, and I delivered you out of the hand of Saul.

"And I gave you your master's house, and your master's wives, into your bosom, and gave you the house of Israel and of Judah; and if that had been too little, I would have added that much again.

"Why have you despised the commandment of the Lord, doing evil in His sight? You have slain Uriah the Hittite with the sword and have taken his wife to be your wife. You have murdered him with the sword of the Ammonites."

2 Samuel 12:5-9, Amplified Version

David had a problem. He went through an elaborate sequence of events to cover-up his problem. Even after it was exposed lovingly by Nathan, David never dealt with the issues in his family. The sins of the father visited future generations. David's family ended up being highly dysfunctional, even though he loved God and was a great warrior. David, like every other person struggling with issues, could not see his problem because of *denial*. It's interesting that David had to deal with the same issues that we face today.

The first cover-up I want to deal with is denial.

I have learned a lot about denial, especially in my own life. When we deny something, we declare it as untrue; thus we don't have to face it or do anything about it. It is a normal human response to situations that carry too much emotional pain for us to deal with all at once. Thank God, I've been blessed to have mature people around me that I am accountable to, that lovingly help me accept reality and properly confront my denial.

Denial is a conscious or unconscious, non-acceptance of the truth. It's not necessarily a willful disobedience; it's a *rejection* of the truth. It's an unwillingness, a refusal, or even an inability to recognize the problems in and around one's self. In the end, denial promotes repression; it destroys trust; and it breaks relationships. I've stated this earlier, but it's worth repeating again: **Denial is one of the largest obstacles to emotional healing.**

No one will ever begin the healing process unless they're able to face the truth.

Isn't it interesting how hard it is to face the truth and to accept something as true or right?

Second Thessalonians 2:10 states that in the last days, people will not love truth anymore. There is an attempt, that is even enforced from the spiritual world, for us to look away from what is true. People in the world refuse to look at truth, and believe that whatever they feel like doing at the time is acceptable. With God, untruth – or denial – is not acceptable. We can deny that something is happening or that something is right, but eventually, truth will catch up to us. It's an inevitable fact. Everything that is covered will be uncovered; lies or untruths will find us out and the truth will have to be revealed. You may have hid a lie or a secret for years and years, but eventually the truth will surface. Truth is too strong – it will always come out. Truth will *always* reign over untruths or denial.

For example, I know people who have had cancer. They deny that they have it, yet are saying that God is going to heal them. They're totally ignoring the fact that the tumors are growing and that they should do what is medically necessary and mix it with their faith. Instead, they're living in this denial thing saying, "God is going to heal me. God is going to heal me." These people are in denial because they're in fear. Yet all the time, they're calling their denial God.

God never said that you weren't supposed to face reality. Instead, all through the Scriptures, He says to name your need, do what you need to do in every phase of it, and He will meet you there with His power.

Denial misinterprets Romans 4:17. Paraphrasing the verse, it says that God calls those things which *do not exist* as though it does exist.

It doesn't say to call those things *that exist* as though it doesn't exist.

If cancer is there, it exists! If it's growing, put down the religious jargon, get the treatment you need, and believe God to meet you there with His power!

Denial not only hurts and seeks to destroy the person it's using, but it also hurts everyone who watches it happen.

Some abused women deny that their husbands are bad because they feel the abuse is their fault. They are in denial about the bad because they choose to remember how good the men can be. A woman like this denies that her needs and self-preservation could ever be important. The man has even manipulated the abused woman to believe that the fault is her own, that something is wrong with her or he wouldn't have beat her up. She is in denial about *his* deep-rooted problem. Denial has been the death of many.

Proverbs 1:7 calls a person who despises truth a fool. We've thought that scripture was only for worldly, unspiritual people. I've discovered that *anytime* we refuse to receive understanding and truth, we are acting like a fool.

Denial is a foundation for all of the cover-ups. It's addictive, much like a drug. There is an emotional pay-off in denouncing reality. Some Christians would shudder and be judgmental towards someone who struggles with a substance abuse issue – yet their own denial mentality dominates *their* lives.

Denial can be the thing that causes people to run for the rest of their lives. Some run openly; others run silently inside, trying to race past the truth. You can read where Proverbs 1 calls out to them saying, "Hey you simple one, why are you running? Why aren't you listening to wisdom? Why are you denying truth?" Denial makes you blind; it declares things better or less harmful than it really is.

Denial can make a person proud saying, "Oh, things aren't as bad as it looks." We can deceive ourselves into thinking it will get better, but there's still no change. "Oh, I don't have a problem at all. Lots of other folks have problems, but I'm doing okay." A month later, a year later, things are still the same or worse. Denial is burying something and trying to forget it; but it doesn't work. Proverbs 29:23 says that pride (denial) brings a man low. As I've stated, truth will always find its way out. So will toxic emotions.

If we are going to receive healing, the first breakthrough will have to come in the area of denial. Sometimes it takes awhile to break the denial mindset, because if we're living in denial, we're in fear. We fear what might be underneath our denial and don't want to face it. Why? Because some of what we're hiding will be difficult to handle emotionally. But you must go there, and God wants you to go there so He can heal your toxic emotions and give you an abundant, wholesome life.

It takes courage to let go of denial. In my own experience of being mentored in this area, I began to understand how denial worked in my life. Only by the grace of God did I realize how *small* it was making me and how *low* it was taking me as a person. Even though it was difficult to name and to face, the Holy Spirit eroded my walls of denial, revealed it to me, and healed the fears and shame that was covered by the denial. Usually, the denial will lie to you so much, that it can be shocking how simple, freeing, and easy the truth really is.

I pray that right now, wherever you may find denial attitudes developed in your life – whether it's your children, your relationships, marriage, church, job, yourself – that God, by His power, would open your eyes to see it. I pray that you will be willing to see the truth, that you will have grace to embrace the truth, and at whatever cost, will hold onto truth as if it were a life-saving device, because it is. It's only the *knowledge* of truth and the *action* as a result of it, that makes us truly free.

BLAME

We live in a society that is addicted to blame. In fact, accusing other people or things for being at fault, permeates our culture. It's so easy to get caught up in the blame game. We blame the weather, blame because we didn't get a good night's sleep; we blame the cat, blame the food – it's just so easy because it's in the air and becomes very acceptable, even "cool" to blame and be a victim!

Some people blame others and hide behind their blame so they won't have to deal with their own actions or issues. People carry offense and blame as a cover for not getting healed.

Blame is a form of self-protection. Another form of blame is projection, or throwing your own feelings forward on to someone else, who might not identify with your feelings, accusations, or actions at all. Blame is also attacking. It is to hold someone, or something at fault. That's actually what Adam exemplified when he said, "The woman, she did it." After the sin, Adam was raw emotionally and spiritually, so he quickly developed a form of self-protection and self-defense. If you had been Eve, you wouldn't have enjoyed it very much.

Adam might have looked tough in his own eyes, but he was really showing his weakness and insecurity in not accepting his own responsibility. Projecting blame means to externalize and attribute to someone else what really belongs to you.

In our soul life, we can become expert blamers. Why? Because it shoves the responsibility on someone else so we don't have to take the responsibility for our own character.

If you carry a blame attitude as a cover, then when you get in emotional turmoil and feel uncomfortable, one of the strategies you use is this – you take the turmoil, turn it inside out, and throw it back on someone else. I've known master manipulators with this problem. If the heat comes on them, they'll always turn it on you – sometimes very subtly and craftily – to make it appear that you have a problem. Some of those who project blame upon others can be very mean, cruel people.

Projection is one of the greatest reasons for conflict and hostility in relationships. One person feels shame, inner pain, or some other intense emotion, and they're not going to own it. How can they if they don't really know or understand what they are feeling? So they attack the other person as a relief for what they are feeling. The blamer may pick a fight, criticize, blame, attack, or confront because the other person has touched the blamer's inner sensitive area.

One of the greatest portions of my healing came when I stopped projecting my blame and my feelings on everybody else around me. I thank God that I was able to be honest with myself in front of a loving God and with the good people around me. Why? Because inner pain from unmet needs, mixed with shame, can produce strong feelings that make you frustrated to the point of doing anything for relief. We think that if other people changed, we would feel better. The truth is, even if other people did change, we would still be miserable if we don't do the emotional work needed to feel better about ourselves!

When I began to heal the shame within me, and my destructive emotions came into balance, I was able to thoroughly examine this behavioral pattern of blame. To put it in real words, I found out that I wasn't as cool as I thought I was. Blame disguises the real problems. Blame hurts *you*. It hurts others around you. Blame is a very selfish way to act, think, and to operate. It hinders you from bonding to God and to others. As we've discussed earlier, blaming delays your healing because you're using all the energy that was meant for your healing, and putting it on someone else. When you choose to change and heal, you will automatically feel better about *others* because you feel better about *yourself*.

The Bible teaches that God is your strength, and through Him you can do all things. It not only teaches that we are new creations in Christ, but that we also have individual responsibility and accountability for our actions.

I spent a lot of time in true, heartfelt repentance. Repentance is a vital key in every aspect of life where we have failed or missed the mark; and it is certainly a key to wholeness. Yet some people refuse to open their hearts and repent.

I believe there is a devil loose, taking advantage of hardened hearts, because in our society – both Christian and secular – people will sue anyone for anything. I've heard of ministers spending their ministry dollars for lawyers to send threatening letters to people they feel are talking about them. Some even twist scripture to do it. It's bizarre.

Something is out of control here; something is a little extreme. We need to investigate our *own* lives, take our *own* responsibility, and take account of our *own* behavior instead of suing everyone and everything that moves around us.

Now there are legitimate situations where that is the right thing to do; but that's not blame. It's done out of lawful justice.

Projection and blame will destroy a marriage. It will destroy relationships. It will destroy children. If you're having a bad hair day, get over it. Don't make everyone else around you suffer because of your misery.

Some will never learn to become the victor instead of the victim, so they continue in the blame game. The emotional wounds under the blame cover-up keep going stronger and stronger in a cycle until there's a crash. And if there is no voluntary repentance, a crash is good.

It's not always bad to hit the wall, because that's the only way some people will face reality. We can read in Luke chapter 15 where the prodigal son had to come to an end to himself. In doing so, he received a miracle. Hitting a wall is not the best way to go because of the all the havoc it causes, but in doing so, the prodigal son returned to his father and was restored.

You don't have to hit the wall and you don't have to be a victim. You also don't have to put up with other people's blame strategies being continually put on you. Rise up! Don't give people power to make you feel a certain way. No one can make you feel a certain way; no one is that powerful! Your feelings are your own and you have to take responsibility for them. Now, another person may stir feelings within you. If that person can push buttons inside of you, maybe you should see if there's a wound you need to heal. But those feelings are *yours*, not the other persons.

Stop the blame and projection. Talk and be real with those you are in relationship with. As soon as you own up to some of your own faults, it will really help you.

It will minister so much to your spirit, and really help relationships when there is conflict if you'll just say, "Hey, I'm really upset with you at the moment, but you are not the problem. I've got to deal with my feelings in this situation." Then step back, take some time, and process. I believe that God honors that decision, and blesses and helps the people who have learned to understand their own emotions.

You are not a victim. You don't have to blame your mate, your co-workers, your colleagues, your pastor, anyone. The problem you're feeling inside is your own. There may be actual circumstances with others involved, but you must take care of yourself and your role in the problem.

Remember, the next time you feel the pressure to hide behind blame and take the heat off yourself, **stop**. Confront how you feel. Manage it, confess it, process it, put it under, and walk in love. Don't use all your motivation to turn the situation inside and out and throw it on someone else.

It's normal to want to protect yourself and resort to blaming others in order to do it. But healing begins when we are willing to *change* ourselves.

CONTROL

Control is another horrible attitude cover-up. The last few years, there has been much teaching in the body of Christ about the characteristics of the Jezebel spirit; but control is not only a spirit. Control is a mentality, a work of the flesh.

There is a positive control, and more people need that in their lives. But control in an extreme fashion will destroy lives and relationships.

Over-control can take many forms. A controlling person may have a powerful presence and a very strong influence. The most obvious is *authoritarianism*, or leading by strong demands.

The general idea is that controlling people organize others to please, protect, and serve them. They do not nurture growth or self-expression among those they lead.

Controlling people are usually strong personalities. Strong people have to be careful not to use that strength or power to camouflage what they have going on inside them.

As a person with a strong "light," I have to be careful not to use my power to control others. I can't use my soulish power so that you won't see that I might not like myself in a certain area. That's what controlling people do.

People use this mask of power for many things. Money is powerful; and if I use my beliefs about money to intimidate and to make me important, then somewhere within, I'm really insecure. Achievements, knowledge, position, and even emotions can also be used as controlling devices.

Some Christians use an anointing or a gift as grounds to control and manipulate others. Let's say for example, if I used extreme control in my ministry, then I would be so absorbed with my **own** dreams that I would cross boundaries invading other people's space, their time, their decisions, the way they work, their personalities, the way they acted and spoke, until **my** vocation, **my** ideas, and **my** expectations crowded out their own identities and personal growth. My life and ministry would then be one of control because I'm so absorbed in my own thinking, goals, needs, dreams, and ideas, that I had no time to focus on attention, love, or need meeting for others. If the person didn't fit into my vision, I would have no time for them.

It is very challenging to learn how to lead without controlling, yet mentoring with authority in the proper place.

It's one thing to have a vision and expect others to follow and support it; it's quite another to use control as a means to secure it. Jesus loved variety and individuality; and He never resorted to the control of others to follow Him, mark His ministry, or to prove He had the message of life and destiny. The basic requirements He had was **to love** and **to believe**. We must give people the space for their own identity and their own growth in the Lord without feeling threatened ourselves. The ministry is just one example; but control in the secular world is just the same. Fear of the unmanageable, fear of failure, unmet childhood needs, loneliness, and shame are all ingredients that produce control and deceive others into being controlled.

Control says that you don't trust others. A controlling person allows others to see what they want them to see and nothing more. Hiding behind this cover-up is a large dose of insecurity. We don't want others to see that we might be weak in some area of our lives; so we come down hard on them with power and control. We think if we can keep others intimidated, they won't get near enough to expose our weaknesses. Controlling people sometimes unintentionally think if their power and authority rules, then it sets up a fortress that others will be afraid to confront. If someone sees through the control, they are immediately shamed and rebuked.

Control damages ourselves, our relationships, our churches, our ministries; our lives. Sometimes a controlling person may see themselves as sensitive and giving, but there is an overly-compulsive thrust to work and get things done. There are arguments, there are separations, all because the controlling person is very nervous that something might be unmanageable, or someone might act out of their rules, spoken or unspoken.

Controlling people are always trying to keep a handle on every thing; on their spouses, their kids, their jobs, their employees. Some try to control every part of their lives. Why? Because if they know they're in control, they can control their pain.

It's not easy to let go of things. If controllers let go, then they feel uncomfortable and out of control, and they might have to deal with their own pain. That is the best thing that could happen to someone with this problem!

There are many, many things about life that are beyond our control.

You might ask, "Well, if I'm not in control, who will be?"

God. God is in control and we are not. Sometimes that's a hard truth to understand and accept.

He wants us to live a life that is free from trying to control what happens to us, and from trying to control others around us. If you recognize the control that's operating through your life, or has been used against you in any way, don't stop there. Go down to the pain, and find out why it's so important to feel that you must always be the one in power and control. If the exploration sparks upsetting feelings that you can't handle yourself, go out and get some help. God wants you free so you can relax and enjoy your life.

If you'll do that, you'll have victory. When you no longer have the hurt and the pain, you won't have to control.

HAVE YOUR FIG LEAVES BEEN EXPOSED?

Have I exposed your cover-up or a cover-up that you have recognized in someone else?

Some have wrongly believed that they didn't need emotional healing unless they were alcoholics or drug addicts. You may not be into substance abuse; but what are you using to medicate and cover your own internal pain and difficulties? It would be foolish to say that you didn't have any covers, because we all do. Some have mastered them so that they are not destructive, but others need both the cover and the toxic emotions touched and healed by God.

Why do we hold onto these shields? Toxic shame is one of the internal issues that needs to be healed; but the covers are the things that the Holy Spirit is working the hardest to pull back so we can be healed.

When He starts pulling on your "fig leaves," you are going to feel uncomfortable. I did. How was I supposed to act now? I had employed these cover-ups for so long, that I wondered if I might now feel too vulnerable.

It was at that time that God reminded me of how much He loved me. In fact, the greatest healing that I received was the knowledge of how much my Heavenly Father loved me. Once I knew that, then I could freely let go of all the other things that I tried to hide behind so I could measure up.

God deeply loves me; and He deeply loves you too. I believe that great fruit is going to come from your life because of the light that the Holy Spirit has shed through the chapters you've read. And I believe that a release for healing will be manifested through the chapters yet remaining.

We've come to the time where we stand with fig leaves removed; there is nothing to hide. We can be rigorously honest, open, transparent, trusting, and vulnerable before a loving and gracious God.

Chapter 16

GIVING GOD ACCESS TO YOUR SOUL

Before we enter into the section of this book where God will give you the knowledge of how to receive healing for your soul, I want to give you some preliminary thoughts.

Whatever degree of shame you identify in your life, there is healing for it. It doesn't matter how deep it is, or how many layers of it there are. Sometimes deeply shamed people will have a sense of urgency and desperation, because they've been paralyzed for so long that they feel hopeless. Relax and allow your hope to be rekindled! When God is involved, it is *never* a hopeless situation.

Is it ever too late for someone to become born again? Then it's never too late to be healed from shame and other toxic emotions.

Understand that there is no quick and easy solution to dissolve toxic shame. You may dissolve a shameful incident in an hour or two. But there is no easy and quick solution to dissolve toxic shame, even in a few days. Patience is the key.

Unless God performs a supernatural miracle, no one is healed of a physical disease in a day. Instead, healing must be received and walked out by doing what you can in the natural realm and by believing God in the supernatural realm.

The same is true with emotional healing. In the soulish realm, we have to walk out the issues and believe for God to meet us there.

God could supernaturally and automatically remove it from you. But since shame is a normal emotion within its boundaries, I believe the highest and the best method is when God teaches us how to walk it out. Why? Because those old issues an be challenged again through the normal wear of daily living. When we understand what it is, how we got there, and what to do about it, it's very difficult for unhealthy shame to find another lodging within us.

COMPARING TWO REALMS

For example, in the physical realm, when a deep wound has been healed, the area may always be a little sensitive when touched. But when it's touched, you don't allow it to be wounded again. No way; you immediately protect and cover the area don't you? That sensitivity works for you because you know where the area is and how to keep another wound from happening there.

The soulish realm is the same. When an area that I've been healed from is touched, now I can immediately sense it. I may even acknowledge it to myself and say, "Wow, I felt that." But now, after my healing, I'm aware the area is there; it's not hidden but it's not open for further damage. New boundaries are set, and shame can't enter in whenever it pleases and it can't set up camp there. Because God remained with me and taught me how to walk through my healing, I know what to do when the painful areas are touched. I know how to stop, think, and sort through my feelings before I respond to old issues and any cover-ups connected with them.

You need time to understand the shame in your life and how it worked in you. You need time to understand the appropriate actions and responses.

Few people go straight through the healing. They usually enter a cyclical process. You will probably find yourself going back to God over and over again, reviewing and continually practicing the healing steps along your way. Don't quit. You will win. God will never give up on you.

YOU ARE UNIQUE

Remember also that **the healing process for each person is different**. The way I healed and the way God may heal you could be different. We are each healed differently in the physical realm; the same is true in the emotional realm.

Unlike physical healing, men and women process emotional issues very differently from one another. A man may deal with his issues one at a time, compartment by compartment. A woman may manifest all her issues at once. It may be like a big wave that builds and rolls over; but when it hits the beach, it's done. Don't compare yourself to another.

If you set yourself up to heal as a carbon copy of another, you may be in for disappointment and let down. I've only told you my story to build faith in your heart. *It's not how you process the issues inside of you. The point is that you come through the process.*

Relax and allow God to work the plan that He has for you. When it comes to the healing process in your life, God desires to minister **specifically** and **individually** to you. There have been countless others that have gone on their journey to emotional healing – long before you – and came out on the other side restored and whole.

JACOB

Our God can take the personal tragedies of life and turn them into triumphs. He takes the things that the devil tries to torture us with, and makes them into something very powerful. There are adversities you have to go through, and if you allow Him, God is with you through the process. The Bible teaches this over and over. It doesn't say that you'll go around the fire, you'll miss the fire, or get raptured from it. No, it says you'll go *through* the fire, but you won't get burned. The fire is a purging and a cleansing. God does a miracle in you and you'll come out without the smell of smoke.

Sometimes you might have thought that you were going to be burned to a crisp! You might have wondered if you were going to make it because you saw nothing but fire. In these situations, our character is developed as our faith is being tested and tried. The results come out as fruits of the spirit in our lives, and it can be a very powerful experience if you understand it, and allow it to strengthen your character.

I really understood this when I read the story of Jacob in Genesis 32. Jacob was alone, face down, feeling like he didn't have a friend in the world. Have you ever been there? While he was praying and pursuing God during that very dark time, he met God in a unique way. I won't go into a theological debate on whether it was truly God or an angel; but Jacob wrestled with the divine Being.

The Bible says he wrestled with God *and* man. He was really wrestling with his own destiny. He wrestled with his place in God, and he wrestled with the trials that mankind had placed upon him.

Let's face it. As we journey through life, we will wrestle with things that are not easy to face or easy to cope with. We wrestle and struggle with things we don't know how to deal with. Like Jacob, we wrestle with the things of God and the things pertaining to life. But also like Jacob, during our darkest hour, God will show up to meet us and bless us.

Although the struggle was lonely, dark, and painful, Jacob never gave up; he continued and pursued until he got what he needed. The Bible says that in the midst of his struggles and wrestling, Jacob refused to let go until God blessed him. He refused to back away or to cower down. He refused to go back into his old way of thinking and living. He had come too far, and he was going through to the other side.

At that time he was struck in his hip; and for the rest of his life, he walked with a limp. Although there was great pain in that season of his life, the Bible states he "prevailed." Jacob went through, but he was marked for the rest of his life.

As we go through life, we will acquire battle scars. The scars aren't anything to fear. Instead they can be marks of progress, of healing, and going on. Scars are the victory stripes for winning life's battles. Jacob walked with a limp, but it was a remembrance to one of the most meaningful times of his life. Yes, it was hard. Yes, it was painful. But through that experience, God changed his name from Jacob to Israel; from Liar, Deceiver to Truth. Jacob's inward parts were so changed and touched that he had to build an altar and called the place Bethel, meaning the place where he met God face to face.

In his darkest, most tragic and desperate hour, God showed up and looked him straight in the eyes. What a beautiful illustration and promise to us! To this day, God still calls that great nation as the land of Abraham, Isaac, *and* Jacob.

Don't allow the darkness to deter you. Don't crumble under the feelings of loneliness, hopelessness, or despair. It will seem like it's there to stay forever, but it isn't. Set your focus straight ahead. Pursue and continue to pursue. **God will meet you face to face.**

DAVID, A MAN AFTER GOD'S OWN HEART

I want to introduce a powerful example of biblical, human transparency.

As a biblical character, the life of David ministered to me in a powerful way. We can read the account of his life in many of the major books of the Bible, but the Book of Psalm records his deepest personal feelings. When you begin to understand the concept and design of shame, you will read the Psalm in a different way.

There were times when I read the Psalm and thought that David was a man of unbelief. I see now that David knew that God didn't shame him, so he felt the freedom to talk to Him and bring all of his shameful situations to the Lord. David knew he could be honest before the Lord, and that God wouldn't shame him in return.

Psalm 139 is a wonderful example of David pouring out his heart to the Lord. I want you to specifically notice verse 23. He prays,

"Search me [thoroughly], O God, and know my heart! Try me and know my thoughts!"

Amplified Version

Another word for thoughts would be anxieties. He was earnestly pleading with God to show him his anxieties and insecurities, because deep down inside of him, regardless of how David felt, he knew that God was the only One who could help him. David was placing himself under the spotlight of the Holy Spirit. He earnestly prayed,

"Behold, thou desireth truth in the inward parts: and in the hidden part thou shalt make me to know wisdom."

Psalm 51:6

David understood that God wanted him to be emotionally whole. In being emotionally whole, he would be spiritually whole as well. He knew that God didn't want him to live in denial, or in any other of the addictions and facades that are used to hide pain and shame. He understood that only God could reveal the hidden secrets and faults that he could not see, as well as the hidden truths. He wanted it with all of his being.

That's the beginning of coming into emotional healing. We must drop our hands in surrender and ask God to search us. Emotional healing doesn't come by someone else searching you, or even you searching yourself. It comes when you allow God to search you and reveal your true heart. You must allow yourself to be placed under the spotlight of the Holy Spirit.

That can be scary, because if the doctor said that you had a serious illness, the first thing to hit you would be fear. As people enter into emotional healing, the feeling is the same. They wonder what it's going to be about, and what is going to happen. I have good news for you: You don't have to be afraid to enter into the experience of healing for your emotions. God will release you from fear, because He wants access to your soul. He loves you!

The awareness of the presence of God becomes something very valuable and precious to you during this time. I spoke at the beginning of this book about the love of God for your soul, and how you are safe with the Lord. If you need to read that chapter again, do it.

Understand that God is not asking you to go back and

re-do any healing work that He's already done. He'll clearly show you any areas that need healing. If you've read this book in succession, you're probably already aware of the areas that He needs to touch. He now wants you to begin the healing process.

David certainly knew that he needed to be healed of toxic shame. He had problems in his soul, and it manifested through his life. Those problems manifested in his sexual life and in his family life. He was the leader of a great nation and a great army; he fell morally and then murdered to cover it. But the great thing is that David obtained his healing. How do I know that? Look what he proclaimed in Psalm 23.

"...he leadeth me beside the still waters. He restoreth my soul..."

Verses 2, 3

Many great men in the Bible poured their hearts out to God, no matter how they felt or how ugly their words were. Elijah, the great prophet of God, sat exhausted and depressed under a juniper tree after running from a wicked queen. He lamented to the Lord, "I've had enough; just take my life because I'm no better than my ancestors." Did God fall off the throne? No. God healed his shame and strengthened him.

Job was one of the holiest men on earth, yet because of great loss and depression, cried, "I have no peace, no quietness; I have no rest, turmoil is everywhere around me." Despite the hardships, Job remained faithful to the Lord for his deliverance. God restored more to Job than the man ever thought possible.

Jonah decided to run from the issues in his heart, making him incapable to fulfill the command of God, and was swallowed by a great fish. In the belly of a whale, with weeds wrapped around his head, Jonah decided to settle his internal issues, and in doing so, made a vow to God. God restored Jonah, the whale regurgitated him on the shore – resurrected him – and Jonah hit the beach running to do what God had commanded. It's wonderful to be resurrected! But the seed has to fall into the ground and die – the dark issues in our lives have to be exposed, then dealt with and healed – before they can rise up into a new life.

David and the others prove to us that it's okay to open up our hearts, our minds, and our thoughts to the Lord. Because of David's transparency and hunger for truth, despite the ugliness of his feelings, God called him a man after His own heart.

Now **you** are the man or the woman of the hour. It's your time to be called one after God's own heart.

Chapter 17

THE HEALING PROCESS:
THE UNDERSTANDING PHASE

In this chapter, I'm going to walk you through the first phase of healing. I refer to it as phases, because emotional healing happens in increments, or by one thing building upon another. It is a process. To understand why we find ourselves in a need for healing, we must first do a self-evaluation. This is the time to unveil your inner being. But it's there you will experience self-discovery.

In the last several years, I've done more self-examination than I've ever done in my life. Before we go on, I want to expose several fallacies in the body of Christ that I've discovered through my own self-examination.

I've noticed that when we are encouraged to examine ourselves, there has been a great fear to do so in some Christian circles. Those that fear this type of scrutiny are in great misunderstanding, mainly because of the extremes from the past. Misunderstanding forces many to under-play the symptoms of pain and turmoil, because they fear the results will cause an out-of-control, emotional upheaval. Others fear because they think they are violating scriptures about what Jesus has already done for them. Because there has been such a lack of sound teaching in this area, some Christians only spiritualize problems and expect others to display massive amounts of strength to stuff it inside, or worse, to ignore it. Some people and leaders ignore or down-play it because of the issues in their own souls.

They've never been taught how to deal with their own issues, so they don't feel capable of helping others. If someone is in that condition, you can see where it's much easier to spiritualize it, to ignore it, and even preach against soul healing.

The truth is, if we don't heal the fundamental flaws and weaknesses in our souls, our entire personalities, ministries, and lifestyles can be out-of-control or excessive in one area or another. I've traveled all over the world and have seen the tragic results of those who are ignorant of the issues in their lives. At times I've been very disappointed by what I've seen; yet it inspires me to continue obeying the Word of the Lord and to shine the light of His Spirit on these various deceptions. It inspires me to bring hope and healing to those that are open, hungry, and willing to learn.

Yes, there is a spiritual side to healing; but it is *one side*. We can't receive healing without the intervention of the Spirit; but there are responsible steps and actions we must take as well. The Spirit of God can reveal to you exactly what you need; but **you** must do the work and gain knowledge and understanding of where it came in, why it remained, and how to keep it out!

Remember, the main reasons for inner turmoil fall into the basic categories of unmet needs, repressed emotions, unresolved conflict, and *the devil's harassment*.

Let me say again that we cannot ignore the fact that we have a soul. When our spirits are grieved, we'd be in big trouble if we ignored it. When our physical bodies are in pain, we'd be labeled a "flake" if we denied it. It's time we understand the balance for our emotions and stop fearing the extremes of the past. This is a new time; and the revelation we have for this hour will bring wholeness in every area of our lives. We need to identify the pain in

our souls – our spirits – our bodies – and heal it by any means necessary before we can live a well-rounded Christian life!

I have experienced many stages of healing and deliverance in my Christian life. I know you have too. Let's step to a new level.

The recent self-examination that I've done has produced the greatest growth and the sweetest peace that I've ever known. Although my life and ministry was overflowing the brim, I would never want to go back and live the way I did before my season of self-examination, self-discovery, and personal healing. I want to continue to go forward and be all I can for God.

As you step into this, you don't need to be afraid of anything you might feel or see. As I've said before, **God is with you more than you know.** He's going to remain at your side as I give you the knowledge to work through the issues of shame.

1. UNDERSTAND WHAT JESUS DID

Before we even attempt to heal the excess and mostly acquired shame that hinders our lives and destinies, we must first realize that Jesus destroyed the effects of all toxic shame and other destructive emotions on the cross. He will not ask you to do more than you can handle.

The Amplified Version of Hebrews 12:1 says,

"Therefore then, since we are surrounded by so great a cloud of witnesses [who have borne testimony to the Truth], let us strip off and throw aside every encumbrance (unnecessary weight) and that sin which so readily (deftly and cleverly) clings to and entangles us, and let us run with patient endurance and steady and active persistence the

183

appointed course of the race that is set before us."

The fact that we are surrounded by a great cloud of witnesses that have already proven the truth is one reason to shake off the dark issues of our hearts! But there's more. Jesus knew that what we have buried in the depths of our beings would hinder us. He tells us here that these things will cleverly cling to us and hide where we might not see them, but to run ahead with patience into our individual destinies.

"Looking unto Jesus the author and finisher of our faith: who for the joy that was set before him endured the cross, despising the shame, and is set down at the right hand of the throne of God."

Verse 2

Notice that to be free from these entanglements, we need to do what we can and to keep moving forward, looking to Jesus as our Example and Deliverer. Why? Because Jesus settled the toxic shame issue on the cross. He despised the shame that keeps us in emotional bondage, that thwarts our potential, damages relationships, and keeps us feeling so desperately bad, negative, and fearful of life itself. The humiliation was multiplied as He suffered for something He didn't do. He didn't deserve to die; and He did nothing wrong to have a crown of thorns jammed into His skull causing excruciating pain.

In other words, He scorned the shame. He laughed at the shame of the cross and defeated it soundly. You see, the cross was designed to be a shameful, indignant way to die. It was mainly reserved for horrendous criminals and murderers. Even the location of the cross was designed to be a place of scorn, as it was positioned on the outskirts of the city, by the front gates. It was positioned in that place so the person hanging there could be disgraced and spit at by the inhabitants traveling in and out of the city.

To make the shame toxic, the crucifixion was planned to take place at the busiest time of the year. It was the season between the Passover and Pentecost, and Jewish people from everywhere were coming into Jerusalem to celebrate the feasts. When Jesus gave up His life on the cross, it wasn't done in some secluded corner. Everyone that passed through those city gates saw it and everyone knew He was being crucified.

When Jesus despised and scorned the toxic shame, it means that although He completely experienced it, He didn't allow it to be a part of Him. He didn't let it win. He didn't let the shame of dying a lonely death consume Him and hold Him down forever. When He asked the Father why He was forsaken, the loneliness He was experiencing was a real feeling. But Jesus, although despised, rejected, and outcast, turned the whole thing around and defeated the shame. In fact, one Greek translation says He laughed at shame in the face.

One of the only ways you are going to be healed from shame is to understand that Jesus took it all for you. He took all of the toxic shame, the feelings, and the effects of it, put it back on Himself, and soundly defeated it through His death and resurrection. He shamed shame! He took it so you don't have to!

If Jesus broke the curse of shame, if He laughed at shame, then there will be a day when I can laugh at shame and the effects of what it has attempted to do in my life, because Jesus went there for me. When I open myself up and believe for the healing He died to give me, He goes there with me. He even leads me to the most intimate details of everything that surrounds my shame – especially the very feeling of the shame itself. Jesus is the healer of shame, because He has already broken its power spiritually and has been there experientially. Through it all, Jesus Christ has sat down victorious on the right hand of the Father. There is victory for everyone in Christ. Please don't give up hope!

Because of the price He paid, the cross means everything. When I need healing, I place my hope, confidence, and trust in what Jesus experienced at the cross. The grace is there. My value as a person and my self-esteem are restored in the fact that Jesus went there for me. Now my toxic shame has to go. I can let it go. I receive self-esteem by looking back at the cross and by understanding that Jesus paid a tremendous price for me. I know I'm very valuable as a person. My needs and feelings count. Because I'm assured of my value to Him, I can let Jesus into my experience. I can feel my feelings no matter how intense or dark they may seem, and then I can release them into the safe and loving environment of His presence because He has already paved the way. He knows; He's been there.

2. YOUR FRIEND, THE HOLY SPIRIT

"So do not make any hasty or premature judgments before the time when the Lord comes [again], for He will both bring to light the secret things that are [now hidden] in darkness and disclose and expose the [secret] aims (motives and purposes) of hearts..."

1 Corinthians 4:5, Amplified Version

I've stated earlier that emotional healing isn't something we figure out with our minds. We don't rack our brains, thinking and concentrating, until we come up with the answer to our problems. Although we are responsible for our actions, the Holy Spirit is the one who will direct us to the path He wants us to follow. The Holy Spirit is Light;

He is the Counselor.

The devil thrives in dark places; and if the problem has been hidden, we need the light of the Spirit to reveal it to us. When the Holy Spirit shines His light on the dark and hidden places, He gives the revelation to act upon it. When He speaks, we understand and we know what to do. If we try to figure it all out with our minds, either confusion sets in or we miss something. If that happens, more trouble and heartache will follow. The Holy Spirit is Truth; and if you'll trust Him, He will reveal the hidden things.

Many times we won't know how to start or what to say. Romans 8:26 in the Amplified Version assures us to come before the Lord anyway by promising,

"So too the [Holy] Spirit comes to our aid and bears us up in our weakness; for we do not know what prayer to offer nor how to offer it worthily as we ought, but the Spirit Himself goes to meet our supplication and pleads in our behalf with unspeakable yearnings and groanings too deep for utterance."

This verse assures us that if we'll just be vulnerable and start seeking and talking to the Lord and to others He has placed in our lives, He will hear the yearnings of our heart and will translate it back to us with understanding.

Many times in my self-discovery, I sat and cried at the wonder of the revelation He was giving to me and at the work of a loving God in my heart. Tears are like liquid prayers. Tears are very healing. The Lord interpreted my tears and in return, gave me strength, peace, reassurance, and understanding in my heart. Because Jesus already paid the price for us, and because we are of such value to Him, Hebrews 4:16 encourages us to come boldly to the throne of grace, fearing nothing, so that we could obtain mercy and find grace to help in the time of need. God wants you to come to Him and present your need. He is the only one who can help you and restore you into wholeness. Heaven is open, and the Holy Spirit is ready for you.

In this understanding phase, expect God to speak to your heart. He will speak through your own thoughts and meditations. He will speak through others. He will speak through books. Let your guard down and let your Instructor talk to you about you. It will be very painful at times, but like others before you, you will make it. Listen for Him and receive what He says. Sometimes in the process of self-reflection, you can see where you're at fault. Other times, God has to show you what you can't understand by revealing specific details about why you are like you are, or where you are wounded or deceived. He doesn't condemn you about your faults; He helps you with them. You are safe with Him. He doesn't hurt you when you are wounded, tender, and down. His desire is for you to become whole, not fragmented!

This entire understanding phase is about growth, maturity, and gaining a deep and detailed knowledge of yourself. We will need this knowledge to walk in integrity, holiness, and in health. We will need to grow in it in order to *keep growing* until this life is done. Knowledge is the key. People are destroyed because they have no knowledge about behaviors, wounds, and weaknesses. They don't even know how they really feel or how they really hurt, or why. God wants us to live in the light and truth of all things!

God wants you to look at this understanding phase in a positive way. One of my favorite verses is in the Amplified Version of Revelation 3:19. The verse so beautifully portrays the heart and character of the Lord when it comes to receiving correction and exposure to the pride, ego, and selfish side of our inner self. He says,

"Those whom I [dearly and tenderly] love, I tell their faults and convict and convince and reprove and chasten [I discipline and instruct them]. So be enthusiastic and in earnest and burning with zeal and repent [changing your mind and attitude]."

If you've been hesitant about meeting with the Lord, that verse should change your mind! Not only does He tell you how tenderly and dearly He loves you, but He goes on to say that He wants you to grow in Him by understanding where you've been carnal, childish, or fleshly, and why you've been that way. Then He says to be enthusiastic about it! Be blessed and filled with joy that you, as a son or a daughter of the Lord, are free to find yourself before Him, growing and changing into His image!

Ask the Holy Spirit to give you self-awareness. Boldly ask for the grace and courage to understand what He's shown you. Ask for grace to endure the purging of your emotions. Then begin to analyze it, take mental notes on it, and think about it what He has revealed.

3. BE PATIENT

Remember, God can heal you in a split second. So what takes the time? What is there to be patient about? The patience comes with your *understanding and mentally connecting with the who, where, what, and why of your emotional self.* Those are the areas that take time. It takes patience to gain the revelation to disarm the lies you've believed about yourself through the years. But once you get the understanding you need, God can heal you in a second.

It would be totally fruitless for God to heal you emotionally in some area that you had no clue about. If He did that, then the same thing would happen over and over again, causing great devastation in your life. God is not heartless. He loves you; and by that love, He takes time for you to put two and two together; or to recognize dysfunctional activity that may have been transferred or developed from your family of origin. It takes time to understand your reactions to certain situations, why you feel the way you do, and then to feel the feeling itself. You can't get emotional healing if you don't feel the feeling and allow it to finally pass through you! The passing brings the release and "unsticks the stuck" emotion. What a great feeling to let the toxic shame out! It changes your life.

Once I began to understand the feelings of shame and how it was working in my life, **the revelation of it was as powerful as the healing.** In fact, the healing took the shortest amount of time. The work and the patience came in getting the revelation I needed in order to process and receive my healing and wholeness. To be honest, the patience to get what I needed was hard. But I constantly renewed myself through the Word and prayer, and refreshed myself through the counsel of godly men and women. As I let God into the depths of my heart, the Holy Spirit worked with me. One by one, those areas came to light. Eventually in God's timing, when I could handle it and receive it – I SAW! Sometimes I was shocked, scared, or even recoiled at what I saw; but that in itself began to set me free. I saw it, I felt it, and I understood it. I was able to work my emotions through.

Please remember that if a specific event caused shame for you, it might not take as much time. But if you've lived a pattern of chronic shame throughout your life, it will be the deepest to uproot. It might take a little more revelation and a little more time. Be patient and work through it. Don't give up, don't cave in, and don't ever believe that the Holy

Spirit has given up on you or lost interest. Remember, in your darkest time, God will meet you face to face. There's always a beginning, a middle, and an end; and the end will come. It didn't come overnight and it won't leave overnight; but the toxic shame and bound up emotions will heal! The power of healing is the greatest thing you might ever experience.

4. GET A FULL AWARENESS

It's not easy to deal with shame, and that's why I approach this area very tenderly. As I've told you, shame is a painful feeling. To go through the halls of shame is some of the hardest work you can do, because it's really painful to touch those areas and feel them again. But if you're going to see it, know how it works; if you take it out and look at it again, you're probably going to feel it. Before you begin, you must understand that's the whole point, the entire key to healing and wholeness. The point is not to stick it down or to deny it or act like it's not there. The point is to take it out, to examine it, and come into a full awareness that this true but distorted feeling has attempted to destroy your entire life. Yes, it may hurt; but once you know it's there, God will show you how to go through it so you won't get drawn into the darkness of it again.

Remember, full awareness is something that takes time. It involves God revealing the problem, you looking at it and not denying it; and it involves calling it for what it is. The best way to do that is to look, listen, and observe yourself. Pay attention to your thoughts. Why do you think a certain way, or why do your thoughts lean a certain way? Pay attention to your relationships. Are they fulfilling, safe, and mutual? Do you cross boundaries or allow them to be crossed in your life? Do you trust others? Have you said, "I'll never allow this situation to happen to me again?" Why would you say that? Do you run away from good relationships when it gets uncomfortable for you? If so, examine why you behave that way. Think about how you present yourself to others. Why do you want them to view you a certain way?

Examine other situations in your life. Are you negative, overly-possessive, controlling; do you project blame? Do you have memories of people, places, or situations that make you uneasy or "emotional" inside when you think about them or reflect on them? Once you take these things out of the closet and look at them, you'll soon get a full awareness of the revelation you need. Again, I want to highly recommend three books that are very helpful in acquiring some in-depth understanding of this subject. They will help both men and women do some of discovery work, and explain emotional healing and the process of recovery in a clear, biblical way. They are <u>Secrets of Your Family Tree</u>, <u>For Men Only</u>, and <u>Living on the Border of Disorder</u> (see SUGGESTED READING).

5. NOTICE YOUR DEFENSES

When shame is active, our first reaction is to either defend it, protect it, or hide it. Women, maybe you fly into a rage when a man does something because another man caused shame for you. Perhaps your mother has a drinking problem and it's a shameful and hurtful habit affecting the entire family, so you lie or deny the problem is even there. Maybe you withdraw when someone is showing love to you. Pay attention to how you defend your actions.

If you need to re-read and thoroughly study the previous chapters on covers and masks, do so. Allow it to be a catalyst to help identify the defenses and excuses you might be using to cover toxic shame in your life. Once you decide to be honest with yourself, the Holy Spirit has the expertise to bring the revelation needed to heal it.

6. ACKNOWLEDGE IT AND CHALLENGE IT

Throughout the book, I've stated that shame cannot be healed unless it's acknowledged. Why? Because shame by its nature wants to hide behind lack of knowledge, excuses, covers, denials, fears, and circumstances. Sometimes we don't even know we carry shame until it's exposed; then God works to remove it.

As badly as you might want to, you can't "wish" shame away, nor can you will it away. I know that's painful, but painful things need a remedy before they will go away. If your appendix was so infected that it became chronic, could you wish it away? Of course not! It won't go away until the physician goes in there and takes it out.

Shame that is revealed works the same way. It's a fearful and painful experience to expose any area of shame. It will always be a painful thing in the depths of your soul if something isn't done. Why live your life that way? Once it's acknowledged, then you've given permission to the Great Physician to go in and remove it, bringing you healing and wholeness.

Shame is never addressed unless it's acknowledged. The devil and shallow, religious-minded people will tell you, "Oh, don't acknowledge it; you don't need to feel that pain again. The experience was too deep; you'll never be okay in that area, so don't open it up." They may whisper something like, "No one has ever confessed that before. That's the most depleted and crooked sin that anyone could ever have. What will everyone think of you?" They will probably even say, "There's no need to get so emotional. You've been fine up to this point without going there."

The enemy will do everything possible to get you to keep the shame hidden. He knows that once it's brought into the light, healing comes! It doesn't take much more than a little of God's light and zoom! The entire shame of the incident floods right out of your being! It's wonderful!

Name the shame. That may feel like the worst thing you can do because it can make you feel like you'd rather die than reveal it. And then, by God's grace, allow the Holy Spirit to help you challenge it.

Don't misunderstand what I mean by the word "challenge." You don't attack shame. I know that many have been taught that we should be aggressive about everything and attack, attack, attack! No, not in this case. The shame that has plagued you has caused you to be very tender or very angry. It has affected your entire being. It doesn't need to be attacked; just bring it to the light.

What you should attack is the knowledge of how shame has worked in your life. You should aggressively pursue as much understanding as you can so that wholeness can have its rightful place in your life. Then you can change your learned behavior habits and reactions because of the toxic shame that was there.

What if the entire body of Christ got a burning zeal to ruthlessly examine themselves, and then would own up to *and* change their faults and fears before themselves, before God, and before man? Can you imagine what an awesome presence of humility, tenderness, and love we would have to the church and to the world? Can you imagine how Jesus would be lifted up, and how the new believers would have the freedom to grow and be all they could be in the Lord? Can you just imagine how we would flourish in our personal lives, in our churches and ministries, and in our position as salt of the earth?

I believe God is dealing deeply with the hearts of believers everywhere; and with our motives, desires, and intents. I believe He is healing us deep down inside where before, only a few dared to go. He is asking us to do our individual emotional work. We can and must do it!

Self-examination means fearlessly searching the deep, inward portions of our moral and emotional make-up. It's an inventory that needs to be cultivated in our lives on a regular basis because it will produce positive and lasting fruit. Once this revelation comes, you can then go into the **action phase**.

Chapter 18

THE HEALING PROCESS:
THE ACTION PHASE

You have now come into the full awareness of the emotions that bind you. In examining yourself, you've noticed the defenses or excuses that have kept you in denial. In spite of the pain, you've been honest, and you're calling it for what it is. You're allowing yourself to feel all the emotions connected with shame, including shame itself. By now you've surrendered it to the Lord, and by faith and patience, you're allowing Him to challenge the lies that have kept you in the pits of darkness. Now that understanding has come, you've entered into what I call the **action phase**.

1. GET HELP

The majority of your help will come from God. He is the very first one that we should talk to and confide in. When God comes in, the ugly, dark issues of our lives will be exposed to the light and will be unable to remain in the darkness where they are festering and infectious. Get alone with God and talk to Him about what you have learned about yourself. Tell Him how mad you are. Talk to Him about your sadness, disappointments, and all the other feelings you have discounted. He already knows it all and He still loves you. He's not going to fall out of heaven!

But it's also very important to realize that as a human being, there is a natural God-given desire to talk to others. It's a fallacy when people tell you not to talk to others but to *only* talk to God. Jesus told people to go and tell someone.

God didn't put you on an isolated island. If we were all so spiritual that we could hear God very clearly and accurately, and knew how to wait for the appropriate answer at just the right time, then I could see us *only* talking to God. But let's be real. Although we'd like to, most of us can't hear God in a crystal clear manner, 24 hours a day. He is a relational and interactive God, and encourages you to be the same with others. The other people in your life can be used of God as instruments of healing.

I don't admonish you to go through deep and painful shame work by yourself. Sometimes the memories of an incident are so painful and leave you feeling so vulnerable that you can't handle it by yourself, and you need to talk it out so it can be sorted.

Within a safe environment, talking creates trust and trust opens the door to love and healing. Sharing with others helps us to identify or pinpoint problems. The people and friends that are the closest to you can easily identify your defense patterns and any other behaviors you might have. They can speak truth to you and the pieces of the puzzle fall into place. Maybe you need a mentor, a pastor, a counselor, or a supportive small group.

By not confiding in anyone, we allow ourselves to feel responsible and guilty for things that have nothing to do with us or who we are. By keeping silent, we let what happened to us become a reflection of who we are. As we break the silence, we allow those around us who care for us to continue to love us and stand by us without questioning or judging. When you are in the presence of those who really care about you – or have someone come to you that you really care about – your words can be true, consistent, and merited, especially if you have exercised yourself from all prejudices.

Many times, just a friend being there is the best thing you could ever have. Sometimes just hearing yourself say it out loud brings answers and healing. I've been blessed to have good, safe people around me where I could cry if I wanted to, or just talk and they would listen. Sometimes I didn't even want any feedback; I just wanted someone who loved me enough to listen and care. There is something that is so redeeming within the soul just to know you have been heard and allowed to express yourself.

If good friends and family members can't provide the help you need, then we must take it upon ourselves to find someone to talk with. That someone can be a minister, a doctor, or a therapist. If you can't find a pastor or a Christian counselor who can help you, then go outside the traditional church setting and seek out a secular counselor **who will honor and appreciate your integrity and will not violate your personal values**. There are excellent therapists and counselors available; some even specialize in certain problems. Ask around and even work with a few until you find the one that matches you perfectly.

I want you to understand that the action you must take to receive your healing is of utmost importance. If the church in your area is not equipped to help you, don't let that stop you. This is the time to press full steam ahead, finding the help you need, whether with "spiritual" counselors or with competent, experienced professionals who have the knowledge and tools to help you heal emotionally.

Do you know what I've personally discovered about living in the 21st century? That there's help for everything!

But sometimes we find ourselves living back in the 13th century, isolated in some little world, thinking that if we're spiritual, we shouldn't need any help. That's a lie from the devil!

In addition to my Bible study and prayer, I seek help everywhere I can find it. I read books, I talk to people, and I've submitted myself to both pastoral and professional counseling at different times in my life. Ask the Lord to lead you and guide you to the people who will help you. There may be a pastor who is trained in emotional health and counseling, who understands the healing of toxic shame and dealing with the emotional realm. The great thing about this is that people who have done emotional work will never shame others who need help.

However He chooses to do it, God will bring the help you need if you'll take the steps to get it.

2. TAKE SMALL THINGS FIRST

In the Amplified Version of Exodus 23:30, God gives us a key to building strength and success. He says,

"Little by little I will drive them out from before you, until you have increased and are numerous enough to take possession of the land."

As we do emotional work, layer by layer, we are building strength and understanding for each phase. By taking one step at a time, we'll soon have the complete understanding that will keep future issues at bay.

Remember, the shame you've experienced didn't come into your life in one day, and it might not leave in a day. But one thing is certain; it will leave. Step by step, little by little, area by area, we get healed. One touch of healing will open the door for more healing to come. The Spirit of God will take you one step at a time.

3. REPENTANCE

Once revelation comes and you've processed the defenses and expressions of the shame and toxic emotions in your life, take those things to God and repent for them. Revelation will bring repentance and humility. There is no freedom except you and I repent.

When I saw the chronic, toxic shame in my life, I saw things in my heart that did not please God. I saw where shame caused me to withdraw from people. When I was supposed to help them, that shame caused me to recoil. I discovered that many times I didn't give the help I was capable of giving. I discovered more truth about myself and my life. I saw some things in me that represented my dark side.

You may say, "Well, withdrawal – isn't that a defense, or a cover?"

Repentance allows you to go beyond the cover-ups you've probably used all your life. For me, any withdrawal was a sin against God.

Once I called it what it was, that defense or cover begin to break apart and lose its hold on me. I saw how my withdrawal hurt people. I saw how my denial was proud. Friends, for several days I was under a strong spirit of repentance. When I saw my shame, it humbled me and my heart was broken before the Lord. I realized the shame sometimes connected to the unpleasant, unrenewed parts of my personality, and that I wasn't living a true, honest, sincere life with truth and freedom in my inward parts.

Even though I never intentionally meant to hurt others, once I saw it for what it was, I had to repent because the actions that came out of my shame, unmet needs, and toxic emotions certainly weren't pleasing to the Lord.

If we're not willing to repent, then I don't believe that healing can be complete in our lives. I'm not saying that we should get trapped in the guilt of our actions and be saddened by what we see about ourselves for the rest of our lives. Godly repentance doesn't work that way. I'm saying that in order to get rid of the shame and its consequences in our lives, we have to put our name on it, own up to how we acted as a result of it, and repent. My toxic emotions have caused me to miss the mark. Your toxic emotions have caused you to miss the mark, and God moves through the power of repentance. It's a spiritual law that when activated, totally cleanses and restores us. It's very humbling to be so vulnerable and honest before the Lord. It brings such a tenderness. The freedom from it is almost too great for words. And the self-discovery leads to a tremendous peace about your true identity.

I couldn't believe the incredible awareness I felt of a loving and forgiving God. When I allowed repentance to do its work in my heart, my healing began to come.

4. MEDITATIVE PRAYER

In your private hours, spend that time with the Lord. I'm not talking about spending five hours a day in prayer or becoming a monk. I'm saying that you must cultivate a personal relationship with the Lord by spending time in His presence with these emotional issues, and allowing Him to speak to you, bring revelation to you, comfort you, and to heal you.

When you're in His presence, gently talk to Him about the issues in your heart. Sometimes you just have to begin by crying out for understanding, especially if this is all new to you. Talk about what He's shown you and what you still need to understand. Take everything out of the darkness and present it to Him. Sometimes, when a shameful area is opened, you'll feel the presence of the shame for a couple of days. The reason you feel the presence of it is so that the pain that is with the shame can flow out. Many times there is a release of upsetting (toxic) emotions, sorrow, feelings of loss, and grief. Let these flow out to the Lord; but if it's too much to bear, please get help. I urge any reader who experiences abnormal depression or anxiety to consult a minister or counselor.

When you open up these sensitive issues before the Lord, the experience doesn't have to dehumanize you. After reading this book, it may be different this time. It's okay to feel the emotions, because when you deal with the shame and it heals, the other emotions are allowed to flow normally. You won't get stuck there anymore, because now they have a free channel to move through. It's almost like a baby learning to walk again in the presence of a loving and caring Father.

5. INVITE GOD IN

I want you to read this section very carefully so that you can understand what I'm saying.

How do you truly and honestly invite God in? Once you're in His presence, you allow Him to come in because you're not going to hide behind your defenses any longer. Those defenses were a cover-up, and not only did they keep others out, but most likely, they kept the most important person out – God.

Once you are in His presence, allow yourself to move into those areas where you once had a defense. It might feel scary because you are used to hiding. But go on over into those feelings that are hiding behind the shield. Once you're there, don't hold onto them – **surrender.**

In the midst of the fear, in the midst of the pain, confess with an honest heart and say, "God, here, I let You in. I surrender this to You. I come to the cross and I allow myself to feel everything that is here, and I let it go; I surrender it." Right there the process of healing will begin. The emotions that were paralyzed begin to move out of the place within, and the shame becomes dislodged.

As you expand into that moment, ask Him to heal it.

I sat there in the presence of God and said, "God, here it is. I'm feeling it; it's real and I'm hurting. This is it, it's wide open and I have nothing to hide. I'm tired of hiding behind it, and I want You to take both the cover-up and the pain."

Your carnal nature thinks that God will be revolted by what you are saying and what you're showing Him. He's not. You want to know what I heard God say to me when I pulled back my fig leaves and handed the shame-filled, painful residue to Him? All I heard was, "Oh daughter, I love you so much. I love you so much." Remember, it's only the power of the love of God that can set us free from toxic emotions.

God didn't shame me and He didn't push me away. He responded to me like I was the purest princess He had ever known. I asked Him to lay His hands on my soul, just like I would have asked a preacher to do in a ministry line. And He did it. He filled me with His light. I felt it.

It was the pure, **unadulterated love of God that healed me.** His love transcended all natural boundaries and fearlessly, tenderly – supernaturally – entered into my emotional realm to restore me. My entire being resonated with wholeness.

6. TRANSFORM IT

While you're totally surrendered in the presence of God, open and vulnerable to Him, feeling His love hovering upon you, it's now the time to ask Him to transform the way you've felt.

Without God's intervention, you won't be able to transform the situation to return your toxic emotions to a normal state. It's beyond your doing. What was meant for destruction, God will turn into good. Let His hand stay on the situation. He can totally change the situation and your feelings with it. Ask Him to shine more light on the situation and reveal His mind to you regarding it. You may be surprised at all that He begins to reveal to you. Remember, with revelation comes understanding.

As you believe for Him to transform it, ask for more knowledge with it. The more knowledge He gives you, the further your healing will progress. The process of transformation will bring great liberty, freedom, and joy to you.

7. FORGIVENESS

Forgiveness is vital in our relationship with God and others.

I don't want you to have a misconception about the spiritual law of forgiveness. Forgiveness can be very difficult. Many have believed that it involves *forgetting* what has happened. It doesn't.

In her book, <u>Honestly</u>, Sheila Walsh told of how forgiveness was explained to her. She said, *"Forgiveness does not minimize what has been done to you. Forgiveness does not make the pain go away. Forgiveness does not blot out your memory. Forgiveness is a God-given strategy for dealing with the pain of life."* [7]

Forgiveness was designed by God as part of the releasing process, to be a cleansing to your **own soul**, regardless of what others have done to you. Yes, forgiveness releases others because their actions can no longer play an emotional tug-of-war within your own soul. Forgiveness is for **you**. If we don't willfully forgive, it opens the door for the tormentors to wreck havoc in our lives because we're holding onto resentment and bitterness. We've already discussed the physical ailments that result from a revengeful soul. Criticism can come from being emotionally attached to something or someone, from being unforgiving about an incident. Remember in John 14:30 where Jesus said the devil could find no place in Him? He lived a life of forgiveness!

As I've stated, many stumble in the area of forgiveness because they feel they must forget what has happened. While it's true that you don't hang the remembrance of an incident over someone's head, it's unhealthy to forget what someone might have done. To forget means that you will become a doormat to an abusive person; or that you have not established healthy boundaries between the person and yourself. To forget means that you have minimized an action that someone might need to be held responsible for. It means you have instead, minimized your value and worth as a creation of God.

We must remember the cause and effects of certain incidents; but I believe it's vital to forgive so that our own souls can find freedom and peace. Let me give you some points to help you in that area.

A. Try to understand why the person did the offense against you. Ask the Lord to show you their hearts and the condition of their souls. Doing so can allow you to simply release people through an understanding of *why* they did *what* they did before you have to forgive them. In the person's condition and background, were they helpless to stop doing what he/she did? Did he/she really mean to do it? When you understand your *own* human weaknesses, isn't it better to make allowance for the human weaknesses of others? Once God shows you what the person might be dealing with, sometimes compassion and grace will arise within you. We all make mistakes.

But sometimes people have shamed and degraded us to the point where it's not easy to come to that place of understanding. If you can't release someone that way, then you'll need to go through the process of forgiveness.

B. <u>**Blame the shamer**</u>. If you're going to forgive someone, then you'll have to hold that person accountable. You can only forgive if you hold them responsible for what they did. Call it what it is; say what the person did. Then you're ready to do the next step.

C. <u>**Surrender your right to get even**</u>. You must allow God the avenue to work in your heart until you're willing to surrender your right to get even. In other words, you must agree in your heart to live with the score untied. God will help you with that, and He'll give you peace and satisfaction in it.

D. <u>**Revise your picture of the person**</u>. You can only do that by the grace of God. Why? Because when you are holding resentment, that person can roll around in your mind until he/she becomes a gigantic monster. You loathe their remembrance; you run from their presence.

When the person becomes a monster to you, you've given the entire incident power over you. Although it may be clear that it was a very difficult, tragic, and demeaning situation, it rules you and owns your life by your own decision. Remember, that "monster" is a mere human being, filled with flaws not too different from your own. God can transform the monster in your mind, and reveal to you the truth behind the situation. Once you take back the power you have given that person, it will be easier to let them go.

E. **Allow God to revise your feelings**. Forgiveness is not a feeling; it's an act of faith. Faith believes. If you're waiting for a feeling, it may not come for years. But faith can be immediate. Faith opens the channels for the grace of God – the power of God – to do the work that is needed. Faith agrees with the Word of God, in spite of how we feel. Sometimes we think that God won't hear our cry to forgive others if we don't feel some kind of results from the prayer. Whether we feel it or not, just the mere action of our will, attempting and desiring to line up with the Word of God, brings the Lord great pleasure. As I've said before, faith plows the tunnel for the feelings to come. Choose faith over your feelings.

F. **Accept the person**. Before you freak out over this statement, stop for a moment. You may be wondering how in the world I could ask you to accept a person that has shamed you to the core. Well, think for a minute of how God accepts you. Even today, with all of your shortcomings and ill-feelings in your heart, God loves you. How does He do it? He doesn't accept your sinful behavior; but He still accepts you as a person that He paid a tremendous price for. In the same way, you do not have to accept the behavior of the person, but you must accept the person for the price that Jesus paid for him or her. Only God can bring us to that place where we can voluntarily offer grace to our shamers.

The forgiveness portion of our restoration can be as much of a miracle as the healing part of it. You may not ever be able to speak to the person again in the natural, and you may not be required to. But you can come to the place to where if reconciliation isn't possible, it's not going to be your resentment that prevents it. And if reconciliation does come, God can give you the words and the grace you need to reconcile. God can help you to accept that person, and by the grace of God, offer grace within your own heart towards them.

G. **Forgiveness works by increments**. You may be a long way in your heart from doing any of these steps. That's okay. I've discovered that forgiveness works by increments, one step upon another. It's not always an instant fix, so don't get under condemnation or bondage because you're not there yet. Forgiveness must take it's full course. Sometimes it takes months to get to the place where you're ready to forgive. I've given you sound principles of forgiveness. Now allow God to keep speaking to you and helping you. Don't run too fast to forgive before you're ready; and don't wait too long. Certainly make sure that you don't wait for your shamer to come back to you and repent before you decide to forgive.

Your shamer may not even realize or be remotely aware of how he/she has hurt you. That person may even be incapable of realizing it. What's going on in your heart is not the fault of any person. Remember, no one is so powerful that they can force you to feel a certain way. The unforgiveness is not between you and them; it's between you and God. Forgiveness is a release and a healing for your own soul.

8. SUPERNATURAL HELP

In the action phase, there is always an ample supply of supernatural help. The grace of God, which is the power of God, can supernaturally change any situation, no matter how difficult it may seem. You can call on the fire of God to purge and cleanse the situation. You can plead the Blood of Jesus to reign and cover over anything contrary to the holiness and truth of God. Divine protection is available; angels are there to minister to you and serve you. The Word of God is sharper than any two-edged sword, and is a mirror for our lives. When the Holy Spirit shines light and revelation on a particular scripture, we can meditate on it, speak it and send it out to accomplish the work it is designed to do. We are promised that the Word of God will never return void or empty from what it's designed to do in our lives. God will also help you find good, safe people that He will use in your life as well.

9. MIND RENEWAL

It's totally fruitless to attempt to renew your mind without healing your heart. Healing produces a supernatural love within your heart. Without love, we're compared to a clanging cymbal that makes a lot of noise without any substance. Once shame and toxic emotions have been destroyed in our lives, we'll begin to read the Word in a new way. We'll see scriptures that we've read a thousand times, and it will have a new and deeper meaning. Once those feelings have been dislodged and healed, it's exciting to go back into the Word. It's almost like reading it for the first time. Allow the Holy Spirit to give you new thoughts; then take those thoughts captive and believe them with all of your heart. Speak them out and be changed.

10. BEHAVIOR CHANGES

Behavior changes will come with time; but this time, it will be exciting because you understand what is happening. I love the statement of an author who once said, "We are all works in progress." When the toxic shame and pain has been released, that statement brings peace instead of dread.

Now, when I feel bad feelings rolling around inside of me, I have to pause, think, and refuse to act on them, but to let them pass through. My shame has been healed, and I don't have to go to the place of allowing my emotions to become toxic anymore. I can take myself out of the situation. I can go and pray if I have to; but I have now learned to live a new life, managing my emotions.

In my behavioral changes, I've learned when there are some dangerous relational situations where boundaries are crossed and others still use their cover-ups to bring shame and hurt. I don't have to put myself back into a hazardous situation too soon. If I've understood that perhaps my parents, or other authority figures are connected to an issue in me, then I must use caution when dealing with them. For awhile, I may have to avoid them altogether until I get the depth of healing that I need. No matter what others say, that's okay. When I receive the healing that I need, I can go back to the depth of that relationship.

11. STAY IN THE PRESENT

Most importantly, enjoy today. Don't try to go too far into your past, and don't venture too far into your future. Enjoy right where you are today. Enjoy your life. Relax and seek to be fulfilled in every area. For many of you, it's the first time in your life that you've actually loved yourself. Toxic, emotional shame has kept you on such a roller-coaster, that you had no idea of your value as a person. Now when you praise the Lord, it comes from a new heart, and from a deeper sense of thankfulness and pleasure. Once shame and pain are removed, no matter your age, you'll begin to see what life is all about.

As you've finished reading this book, I know many things have been stirred in your heart. I know for each one of you, it has meant something different. Right now, I want to pray for you.

I release the restoration of hope to come to you. I release the healing of the soul, healing for insecurities, and healing for the emotional realm. I release the anointing to go into the deepest part of your soul, so you can experience new levels where you need them; in your heart, in your mind, in your emotions, in your relationships. I know that the release of this anointing means change; change in your heart, change in your attitudes, a healing from toxic emotions and the pain associated with them, and a deepening of your relationship with the Lord.

I'm thankful that God is helping us to become like He created us to be; vulnerable, open, and unashamed.

I want you to know that I believe a miracle is going to take place in your life. There is nothing we've done that is unforgiveable. Yet the devil tried to put that over on us, and make us employ cover-up strategies to hinder us from being genuine and authentic, tender and touchable. The toxic emotions have not allowed us to be who we really are, and have stolen a lot of time and energy. Jesus has already made the way for us. He despised the shame and pain so we wouldn't have to live under its effects. Praise God!

I encourage you to continue on your journey of self-discovery, as it's a walk we each take everyday, step by step. Others in your life may never change; but you have, and you can change even more. Some may never change; but you have. The results of your healing will dramatically impact the lives of those around you today, and for the future generations yet to come.

May we all come together, grow, mature, and resonate with the sound of wholeness.

AUTHOR'S NOTE

Once again, this is a book about discovery, resolution, and the healing process. My purpose in writing this book is manifold. First, to present a very *simple* message to help interested people to start on a path of self-awareness leading to emotional healing. I am not a front-line clinician, and don't claim to be. I have written in a non-clinical way, intended to be useful and informative for the everyday believer.

Secondly, I have written to help legions of God-fearing Christians who know they are suffering with some sort of emotional symptom, find what they need to heal toxic emotions and the bondages that bind and influence their lives.

Thirdly, I have written to the Christian community with the hope that a knowledge and awareness of the importance of emotional soundness will come to us. I exhort the Christian church, especially charismatics, to be open to get the understanding we so desperately need.

You don't have to agree with the entire book to find some parts pertinent. You don't have to agree with any of it. But my prayer is that people find the nuggets they need to heal.

I am aware that in our faith community it can be controversial to talk about emotional health, especially if there is any perceived inclination toward psychology, therapy, or professional counseling. In some cases, Christians can be intolerant and judgmental against people seeking the answers to their emotional questions. We get scared at the phrase "inner healing." The fear of "psycho babble" and secular humanistic theories replacing God's Word and basic Christian values become a paramount issue when we openly discuss emotional health issues.

Chuck Swindoll states in the Foreword of the book, <u>Secrets of Your Family Tree</u>, *"As we find ourselves in the last decade of the twentieth century, the painful truth has finally been allowed to come out of the closet. At long last, pastors and congregations alike have stopped whispering and started addressing the secret struggles that plague many, if not most, families. Rather than pounding pulpits and demanding instant change, we have discovered that dysfunctional families are often in the church, and that recovery takes time and is a painful process, and, in fact, that the process cannot be accelerated by cramming more and more convicting scriptures down the throat of the abandoned or the abused."* [8] He went on to say that it was doubtful that books that are straightforward, dealing with emotional healing, would have even been published fifty years ago. If they had been, most in the church would never have read it. I'm glad times have changed!

Basically, I am writing from the simple but direct premise that there is healing available for toxic emotions. Some readers may find that healing toxic emotions can spark some upsetting feelings and some emotional upheaval. For the person who experiences abnormal depression or anxiety, or who just simply wants more help in this process, I recommend finding an *effective* counselor, whether it be a pastor or a professional. If necessary, part of the help for hurting people can come by talking to a safe, supportive, mature, and knowledgeable SOMEONE.

Some are at a point where they can't just will their way out of their feelings, or pray their way out of it, or "pull themselves up by the boot straps" out of it. They need assistance. We can glean from the experts. The study of human emotion and behavior has some helpful ideas, observations, illustrations, and generic methods with which to communicate God's solutions for man's problems. God has many different avenues of getting healing to us. We need to use them all.

I encourage believers who have internal struggles and issues in the soulish realm to get the help they need, even if it's outside a traditional church setting. They don't need to be ostracized because they are depressed, or cast out because they need medication or some specialized time and care to achieve peace and victory in the struggles of life.

Fortunately, my experience with counselors and therapy both personally and as a pastor have been *very* positive, and I have seen dramatic changes in people's lives, including mine.

Let me state what I **don't** advocate. Christians should never trust only in psychology or replace it for God, His Word, and church life. I don't believe that *everyone* must turn to special experts for help, or that *everyone* needs a therapist unless they are led of the Lord. But God *does* lead people to do deep, emotional work.

I also don't believe that there is any problem that is too severe for the Bible, but sometimes we need additional insight to assist us in experiencing biblical truth.

Furthermore, no counseling experience, whether pastoral or professional, should have anyone so preoccupied or involved with problems for years on end with no hope of being healed. Nor should any counselor use weaknesses against their clients to exploit them in any way, like some experienced with pastors in the 70's Inner Healing Movement, or with some unsafe professionals.

I want to protect Christians from getting poor help, yet encourage them to be open to get the quality help that is available in today's world. Our Christian community needs to open up at large, to the beneficial principles that emotional health has to offer – whether the ministry is done by "spiritual" counselors, or competent experienced professionals with a psychology background, or sparked by a book like this.

Finally, no counseling or therapy experience can be complete, no matter how good it is, without the needy, hurting person taking **personal action** derived from God's Word. Any problem that is discussed and revealed must be subjected to and combined with prayer, repentance, the Scriptures, forgiveness, obedience, and the anointing to achieve full healing and deliverance.

In the end, there isn't one answer except that God, by the Holy Spirit, shows you truth, the source, and the reality of your situation. He then helps you heal by applying biblical principles, thus releasing God's power for victory in your life.

If God explicitly directs you to find a good counselor, I recommend you read How to Find the Help You Need, by Dr. Archibald D. Hart and Dr. Timothy F. Hogan. This book gives a detailed explanation to help you make informed choices.

As I've stated in this book, and one person so beautifully put it, "we are all works in progress." When life breaks our hearts, we need to turn to God to heal it. We need not fear suffering, nor do we need to dodge our emotions. When we cooperate with our experiences in the affairs of life, they can bring growth and a deeper healing experience. They can create more character and reveal more of God. Clearly we are at a time when our community needs to heal, grow-up, and resonate with the wholeness and soundness only God can give. I encourage you to give yourself the chance to heal toxic emotions, and find your true identity.

If you are interested in having Mary Alice Isleib speak to your church, organization or special event, please contact:
Mary Alice Isleib Ministries
P. O. Box 44490, Eden Prairie, Minnesota 55344
(952) 942-1877

To receive our free newsletter, or to order other ministry products by Mary Alice Isleib, including her international best-selling book, *Effective Fervent Prayer*, contact us at the above address or phone number.

SUGGESTED READING

- **Healing For Damaged Emotions**
  by David Seamands (Victor Books)
- **Why Do Christians Shoot Their Wounded?**
  by Dwight L. Carson (InterVarsity Press)
- **Thought Warfare**
  by Cindi and Richard Rhorer (Two by Two Ministries) *
- **Honestly**
  by Sheila Walsh (Zondervan)
- **Healing The Shame That Binds You**
  by John Bradshaw (Health Communications, Inc.)
- **Living On The Border Of Disorder**
  by Cherry Boone O'Neill & Dan O'Neill (Bethany House)
- **Released From Shame**
  by Sandra D. Wilson (InterVarsity Press)
- **Boundaries**
  by Townsend Cloud (Zondervan)

- **The Secret Life Of The Soul**
  by J. Keith Miller (Broadman & Holman)

- **Compelled To Control**
  by J. Keith Miller (Health Communications, Inc.)

- **Secrets Of Your Family Tree**
  by D. Carder, Dr. E. Henslin, Dr. J. Townsend, Dr. H. Cloud, Alice Brawand (Moody Press)

- **Love Is A Choice**
  by Dr. R. Hemfelt, Dr. F. Minirth, Dr. P. Meier (Thomas Nelson)

- **How To Find The Help You Need**
  by Dr. Archibald Hart & Dr. Timothy Hogan (Zondervan)

- **The Silent War**
  by Henry J. Rogers (New Leaf Press)

- **For Men Only**
  by Dr. Ted Roberts (East Hill Church, P. O. Box 650, Gresham, OR 97030)

* For this particular book, contact the office of Mary Alice Isleib, at (952) 942-1877 for ordering information.

FOOTNOTES

1. Taken from <u>The Secret Life of the Soul</u>, by J. Keith Miller, Broadman and Holman, copyright 1997. Used by permission.

2. Taken from <u>Healing for Damaged Emotions</u>, by David Seamands, Chariot Victor Books, copyright 1991. Used by permission.

3. Taken from <u>Facing Codependence</u>, by Pia Mellody, Harper Collins Publishers, copyright 1989. Used by permission.

4. Taken from <u>Facing Codependence</u>, by Pia Mellody, Harper Collins Publishers, copyright 1989. Used by permission.

5. Taken from <u>Secrets of Your Family Tree</u>, by D. Carder, Dr. E. Henslin, Dr. J. Townsend, Dr. H. Cloud, Alice Brawand, Moody Press, copyright 1991. Used by permission.

6. Taken from <u>For Men Only</u>, by Dr. Ted Roberts, East Hill Church, copyright 1993. Used by permission.

7. Taken from <u>Honestly</u>, by Sheila Walsh, Zondervan Publishing House, copyright 1997. Used by permission.

8. Taken from the Foreword as given by Chuck Swindoll in <u>Secrets of Your Family Tree</u>, by D. Carder, Dr. E. Henslin, Dr. J. Townsend, Dr. H. Cloud, Alice Brawand, Moody Press, copyright 1991. Used by permission.